THE GENTLEMAN:
A DYING BREED IN AMERICA

A MUST READ FOR

MEN Who Think They Know What Women Want

AND

WOMEN Who Want to Understand Why Men Think This Way

Never accept less, tha you deserve!

JEFFREY A. WERTZ

ISBN: 978-1-5356-0913-5

Acknowledgments

To my mother, Shirley Edmiston, a heartfelt thanks for making me the man I am today. Your strength over the years has earned the love and respect of all who know you. When most women would have faltered, you grew stronger.

A special thanks to Akemi Murakawa and Shelley Hopper for their important role in helping me put this book together and making sure it made sense. Without your help, this accomplishment would not have been possible.

I wish to thank the following people, who have contributed directly and indirectly to this book. Thank you, Jennifer, Natalie, Chelle, Dee, Monique, Winnie, Maria, Esther, Elizabeth, Angela, Sheryl, Barbara, Kristie, Michon, Janine, Monica, Edwina, Diane, Nancy, Justin, Don, Matthew, Keith, Paul, Robert, Scott, Tommy, Eric, Jeff, and Rich.

Last but not least, I would like to thank all of my new friends from the international community, who provided information concerning the countries mentioned in the book. Thank you, Chen Juxian, Bente Solberg, Petra Ochs, Kyong Hui Yu, Nattanicha Yapa, and Nantiya Chaiyuak.

Contents

Preface

CHIVALRY AND THE ART OF being a gentleman are disappearing from America, and it is time we do something about it! I am not a psychologist or a behavioral specialist, nor am I an expert when it comes to relationships. I am an average man, but a gentleman. A man who simply believes that there is a certain way to treat women, in personal relationships as well as in everyday life. I guess you can say that it is a passion of mine.

I have noticed the disappearance of basic etiquette and manners over the years and have often considered putting my thoughts on paper. It all happened very casually. I happened to be visiting my son for a few days and we began discussing this issue. Like me, he is aware of and practices proper etiquette. He mentioned that he is the only one of his "group" that does so, and that he is sometimes made uncomfortable by this. I told him that even though his friends might joke with him, he can be assured that the girl he is with is very aware of his actions and so are the dates of his friends. Upon returning home from visiting my son, I brought up the issue to some friends, which led to hours of conversation about the disappearance of the gentleman in our society. It was interesting because every person, regardless of sex, age, or background, agreed that manners and etiquette were things of the past. Everyone offered reasons as to why, but I didn't agree with any of them. A few days later, I was sitting in a restaurant, writing down some thoughts. A young woman sitting next to me asked what I was writing and I told her about my discussion with my son and friends and that I was thinking about writing an article about how men treated women today, compared to a few years ago. Her mother, who was sitting next to her, heard my comments and walked around, sat on the other side of me, shook my hand, and said, "Thank you, it is about time someone wrote about this because it is so true." The three of us then engaged in a two-hour conversation on the subject. It was quite interesting to hear the points of view of the twenty-five-year-old college student and her fifty-year-old mother. It was at this point that I decided that a single article would not be enough, and that something longer would be necessary to cover this issue thoroughly.

While doing my research for this book, I spoke to approximately one hundred men and women from different parts of the U.S., as well as many men and women from other countries. They all provided valuable insights into how men treat women in America, as well as in other countries around the world. As you will see in the book, I not only discuss my view on the disappearance of gentlemanly behavior, but also provide some basic manners that men should perform with women. I provide the views of a number of other men and women, and even have a chapter with input from women from other countries, explaining how men treat women in other countries in comparison to the U.S. Last of all, I talk about the way ahead and what needs to be done to reverse the current trend. It is a short book; the message is strong and contains concepts that transcend time. I hope readers, men and women, get something from this book that results in better treatment and higher expectations when it comes to the way men treat women.

1.

The Gentleman

Gentleman: A civilized, educated, or well-mannered man.

BEING A GENTLEMAN IS NOT all about opening doors, pulling out chairs, and treating women with dignity and respect; it is far more than that. You can almost say that being a gentleman is a way of life. It can include the way you walk, the way you talk, the way you carry yourself, and, of course, the way you treat others, both men and women. It is not necessarily as much about etiquette as it is about treating others with dignity and respect. Age, social status, appearance, etc. should not make a difference in how a gentleman treats another person. He will always act in a respectful manner. Showing proper etiquette in the presence of women is only one part of being a gentleman, and what I concentrate on in this book.

Where have all the gentlemen in America gone? Why is it so difficult to find anyone under the age of forty who treats a woman with proper manners? Why is proper etiquette, when it comes to interacting with a woman or even behavior in general, now an exception and not the rule? I hear so many excuses from men about why they don't treat women like ladies anymore, and as far as I am concerned, they are just excuses to be lazy, not to put forth a real effort to show a woman that they care and are interested in getting to know them.

For instance, I am sure almost everyone has heard at least one man say that women don't want to be treated specially, that they are fully capable of taking care of themselves and prefer to be treated as a man's equal. By the time you finish reading this book, you will see that logic is simply not true. The first thing I ask a man who makes those comments is, "Has a woman ever prevented you from opening a door for her or pulling out her chair?" The answer is always no. I have dated for many years, been in serious relationships and have even been married, and in all of my relationships, I treated the woman with what I consider to be proper etiquette and respect. I cannot recall a single incident when a woman rebuked me for attempting to perform common courtesies, such as opening the car door for her or helping her with her coat. Granted, there are some things that you might perform specifically for a date (which I will address later), but a gentleman shows these small gestures to all women. I am not saying there are not any women out there who would not say no, for some reason or another, but I am saying that they must be few and far between, because I could not find one.

During the interviews I conducted while writing this book, many women said that they expect a man to be a gentleman and treat them as a lady. The majority of women said that though it is not necessary, it is certainly appreciated, and it goes a long way in their decision to go out with the man and a long way toward a positive first impression. I had a few laughs when some of the younger men I interviewed referred to the feminist movement and women wanting to be treated as equals, because the truth is, in most cases, the younger generation has no idea what the feminist movement was/is all about and just repeat what they heard from someone else; it is just an excuse for being too lazy or simply not caring to show proper manners and etiquette toward women. These men equate the feminist movement to treating women as equals in social situations, rather than taking time to learn the real issues of the feminist movement, which were much deeper: equal pay for equal work, sexual harassment, sexual violence, reproductive rights, etc. I went online looking for pictures and footage of protests concerning women's rights and equality, and although there were many articles and pictures to be found, I could not find a single sign that said, "Don't be a gentleman," "Don't pull out my chair," or "Don't open my door."

Women certainly want equality in many important areas, but the right not to be treated like a lady is not one of them. The point is, don't assume that a woman you are with does not want you to open a door for her or help her with her chair. Make the attempt, and if she does not want your help, she will let you know. I think it is a very safe bet that you will not be turned down very often, if ever. You cannot go wrong by attempting to exercise proper etiquette and showing good manners when in the presence of a woman. The worst thing that could happen is that she says no, but even then, she has mentally made a note that you were willing to be considerate. By not even making the offer, you may never have another opportunity to take that particular woman out again because you did not meet her expectations; or, in the event of a business setting, you could lose a chance to close the deal because of the impression that you left her with. Treating a woman with kindness and respect is one time that being an overachiever can only help you. Perceptions and first impressions go a long way, both personally and professionally. If you don't know how to conduct yourself in certain situations or just refuse to conduct yourself according to the situation, then you can only blame yourself for any negative ramifications for your actions or inactions.

Another excuse that I heard fairly often from members of the younger generation is that it is embarrassing to perform certain basic polite gestures for their girlfriends, female friends, and even female business associates, because none of their friends or other men their age are doing it. This is just another poor excuse for not showing someone you are willing to perform those little special things that show you care. I think these young men should be looking at it from a completely different point of view. A gentleman is confident in himself and doesn't care what others think. He will look at this as an opportunity to show his good side, which will most likely impress the woman he is with. In the case of a girlfriend, this is a chance for a man to show that she is special, and because of that, he is willing to embarrass himself in front of his friends by doing things his friends don't do for their girlfriends. Therefore, his actions mean even more to his girlfriend, if she is the only woman being treated that way. It allows her to look at the other women in the group as if to say, "Look how my man treats me." As I stated earlier, there are no negative impacts to acting like a gentleman, but the benefits can go a long way.

I remember when I was young, I watched old black-and-white movies on television, noticing how just about every man on the screen treated women with dignity and respect, paying special attention to her and treating her like a lady. It didn't matter if the man worked in a factory or was a high-class lawyer; he treated women with respect and showed proper etiquette. I think it was because of these TV shows that I grew up thinking it was normal for a man to behave in a particular way toward a woman. In the old movies, it often appeared that the women reacted more positively to the men who treated them well, through simple acts and special attention, than to the men who tried to impress them with expensive meals or gifts. Maybe the old adage "you get what you pay for" applies in this case.

I always assumed women preferred a gentleman, because it required more of an effort to show affection than it did to just throw money around and not put forth a true effort. Remember, it costs absolutely nothing to behave like a gentleman, but the return on your actions can be very valuable and can have more of an impact on a date, friendship, or business relationship than any expensive meal or gift. There are some women you can impress or buy with money, but in most cases, that does not lead to a healthy long-term relationship. In my conversations while I was writing this book, most women stated that they are looking for a man who treats them specially and makes them feel protected and secure. As a matter of fact, these two qualities came up time and time again. The general trend from the women who are truly looking for a long-term relationship is the desire to feel a sense of security and safety. The majority of women who talked about these qualities feel that the men who show proper etiquette tend to be the men whom they are drawn to and picture being with. It is nice for someone to splurge and spend big money, but in the long term, they want the man who can make them feel special.

As I mentioned earlier, while growing up, I thought it was normal for men to treat women as ladies, performing simple acts of kindness, such as opening doors, pulling out chairs, or even helping with their coat. Therefore, as I began dating, I copied those same gestures. It was quickly obvious that the way I treated women was not the norm, because I soon noticed that the women I went out with were quite surprised and sometimes actually speechless. I received many nice comments and thanks from the women, regardless of whether it was a date or just a female friend.

Most of the time, the women made complimentary comments such as, "It is nice being around a gentleman," or that I made them "feel like a lady." They appreciated the attention they received because it truly made them feel they were special. I began to learn more about what was considered proper etiquette, going as far as asking female friends of mine what they liked a man to do for them. The answer was always the same and is mentioned throughout this book. They stated that they wanted the man to show confidence and not be ashamed to treat them like a lady in public. They liked a man who opened their door and pulled out their chair. Simply put, they wanted to feel special. It was also nice knowing that I was responsible for bringing a smile to a woman's face simply by treating her with courtesy and respect. It made me feel good to make another person feel good about themselves. I have to admit, even back then, I felt a bit conscientious, because although most older men were treating women in a similar manner, most of the kids my age did not, so I opened myself up to some jokes and name-calling. But the truth is, it just felt right to me, so from a very early age, I treated women I came into contact with as ladies. It was during this timeframe that I gained confidence and became the man that I am today. Being courteous to women became a normal part of my life, and I actually found myself paying attention to other couples to see what other men did to make a woman feel special.

During my late teens and into my early twenties, as my social life began to expand, I noticed there were still a number of men who treated women the same way I did: opening doors, pulling out chairs, helping them put on and take off coats, even lighting cigarettes, etc. But sadly, as I grew older, it became very obvious that the number of men who treated women this way was declining dramatically. The number of men who were not ashamed or embarrassed about treating a woman specially by paying attention to her or showing he was proud to be out with her was decreasing. Eventually, as years have gone by, it has gotten to the point that you can actually sit in a restaurant for hours and not see a single man under the age of forty show any signs of "proper" etiquette. Fortunately, you will still see some older couples come in and the man will pull out his partner's chair or take off her coat, but it all appears to be lost on the younger generations.

Take a look at some dating sites and read the most common words on women's profiles: looking for a gentleman! A large amount of profiles on the dating sites very clearly state that they are looking for a gentleman, a man who knows how to treat a lady and will make them feel safe and secure. During my search of the sites, I could not find a single profile where the woman says that she is looking for a man who is oblivious to her needs and doesn't have any knowledge of how to be respectful to a woman. If women truly don't care about how they were treated by men, you would think they would just say so and increase their odds of finding someone. The fact is, they do care, and they are telling the men exactly what they want and how you can win them over. If they state this in the very profile they are using to find a partner, isn't that evidence enough that they want to find a gentleman who can treat them as a lady?

I often wonder if having a class in the schoolroom on proper etiquette and how to treat women could help the youth today. In some cases, they are mentored at home by their parents, but what about those who do not have the same opportunity, who do not have a male role model and were never made aware of proper etiquette? If you are lucky enough to have parents who teach you manners and proper etiquette, the odds are you will perform the same acts as you grow older and are involved in social situations. However, if your home environment is one where you do not have the opportunity to see proper etiquette, then you would not know how to behave in different social settings. The same applies to the expectations of women. Those women who grow up in a household where the father treats their mother with proper respect expect the same when they begin dating, while those who do not have much lower expectations. Therefore, a class on etiquette or manners, mentoring from another father figure, or books such as this would be their way to learn. If it is not being practiced at home, then a young man may not have the opportunity to learn the behavior. So wouldn't it be nice to have a class that enables all children at a certain age to learn ways to show respect to women and people in general? In the past, such classes were not necessary, but as you look at society today, and view the way people treat one another, maybe something as simple as a mandatory class in school could help bring back the days of proper etiquette.

During my research, I found myself shaking my head in bewilderment as I read articles from other authors on this same subject. I read various articles about why men treat women specially and found comments such as: showing etiquette or showing manners to a woman is not a good thing, and is considered sexism, and makes women feel weak and feel as if they need protection. What an absurd thing to say! Is it really so hard to believe that men treat women with dignity, and respect, and show proper courtesies and etiquette because they want to make a woman feel good or just bring a smile to her face? Is it so hard to believe that a man treats a woman nicely to simply show that he cares about what they think about them? To make a general statement to say it is bad is absolutely ludicrous. Not only does it say that men are incapable of treating a woman right without having a hidden agenda, but it also says that women are wrong for wanting to be treated specially by someone they care about.

As I mentioned at the beginning of this book, I am not a psychologist, a behavioral specialist, or an expert when it comes to relationships, but I don't have to be an expert to know that nothing is wrong with wanting to treat someone specially, and nothing is wrong with wanting to be or feel special, and to say that either of these is wrong is simply absurd. I assume that the writers of such material have had their own bad experiences, or talked to people who have had bad experiences, and now group everyone into one category in order to sell their theory and/or articles/books. It goes without saying that there are men who have their own agenda when treating a woman nicely, especially someone they have just met, but they are few compared to the number of men who truly want to make a good impression. It is not bad to do the right thing at the right time. Letting a woman know you care about her by doing little acts of kindness can make a difference in establishing a relationship and is not bad. It is this type of mindset that has aided the disappearance of gentlemen in our society.

When it is all said and done, the only reason a man would not want to show a woman proper respect, especially someone he cares about, is ignorance.

2.

Proper Etiquette

Chivalry: Showing respect and politeness, especially toward women.

It appears that chivalry has morphed from a system of values such as loyalty and honor, which knights in the Middle Ages were expected to follow, to nothingness. It has been a slow change, but the misunderstanding of events such as the feminist movement has brought us to where we are today. Unfortunately, the youth of today don't know what they don't know. Not having role models to show them proper manners and treatment of women has resulted in the younger generations treating women in a way that women do not expect or want, putting the average man at a disadvantage in comparison to those few who have had good role models.

In order to be able to treat women with the etiquette and manners that most of them expect, you have to know what those expectations are and the proper way of performing them. In this chapter, I will list and discuss some basic etiquette that you might want to consider, not only with someone you are dating but with women – with people – in general. It might help you to read the information provided with each example. I hope that maybe it will help you understand how to perform these little acts of etiquette, which could benefit you sometime in the future.

Open all doors (including car doors) – Try to always open the door for women. It does not matter if it is your date or just someone who happens to be going into a building at the same time. It doesn't even matter if she is a complete stranger. Try to put yourself in a position that allows you to easily open the door without reaching across or above her head, or in a way that could lead her to think you are making an inappropriate gesture. This applies to car doors as well. You should always open the car door for your date, making it easier for her to get in and out of the car, but it is also a nice gesture toward any woman. This is especially important if they are wearing clothes that make it difficult to get in and out of a car. Opening doors used to be the most basic of courtesies, but as I began writing this book and talking to women, it became obvious that even this basic gesture is becoming a thing of the past.

Help take off and put on coat – It is a nice practice to help a woman take off and put on her coat, especially when she is wearing a long coat that is more difficult to manage. This is also an important gesture if you are in a tight space such as between restaurant tables or seats at a movie. Something else to consider if you are helping a woman with her coat is how to manage her long hair, because it could get trapped inside her collar. If so, gently lift her hair from underneath the coat collar and lay it over the back of the coat. Most women will give you extra points for even knowing about this courtesy.

Pull out the chair – Another very basic gesture you can perform for a lady, whether she is your date, a friend, or a business associate, is to pull her chair out when she is ready to sit down. You should always pull out a chair for your date. In some restaurants, the host will attempt to pull out her chair, but you can intercede and do it yourself. In the event that you are with a female friend or business associate, it is okay to allow the host to pull out the chair. When you are pulling out the chair for a woman, it is important to pull it out far enough from the table to allow her room to move between the table and chair, and as she begins to sit down, slowly move the chair forward, allowing her to sit into it. If you are at a restaurant, club, or another facility where one side of the table is a padded bench and the other side is a chair, offer the woman the inside padded bench so that she does not get bumped around by other customers and staff. If she says she prefers the chair, then pull it out for her and take the padded seat yourself. As you leave, if she is sitting in a chair, you should go around and pull out her chair, making it easier for her to stand up from the table. I assure you, no woman wants to scoot her chair backward a few inches at a time while she is in a dress, long or short, trying to get enough room to stand up.

Find out what she wants to order and order for her ("The young lady will have…") – This is not done often, especially at family-style restaurants. However, if you take a date to a fine-dining restaurant, there is nothing wrong with asking what she would like to order and, when the waiter asks, ordering for both of you. If there are follow-up questions, she can answer. This is not necessary when you are out with a friend or at a business dinner.

If there is a bottle of wine or water on the table, keep her glass full – Pay attention to her glass. If she is drinking wine or water and there is a bottle on the table, keep her glass filled. If you notice her glass is almost empty, ask if she would like some more and, if so, fill it for her. Don't wait until she has to ask or she starts to fill her own glass. We all know that she is quite capable of filling her glass, but that is not the point. It is the thought and the gesture that matters.

Walk along the curb and keep her on the inside – When walking on the street, walk along the road to protect the woman, in case a passing car splashes mud or dirt. It also keeps her away from bicycle paths and other possible dangerous situations. There are exceptions to this: for example, if you are in an area with ongoing construction, you might want to walk to the inside, where there is more dirt and dust. I did not realize how many women looked for the man to separate her from possible danger or discomfort. Many women mentioned this issue during the interviews, making it very clear that they noticed when men walked on the side that "protected" them.

Do not walk ahead of the woman; keep even with her – It is amazing how often you see men walking one or two steps ahead of the woman with whom they are walking. Pay attention to the woman you are with and walk beside her. Act as though you are with her and are enjoying her company and the conversation. Most women consider it very disrespectful to walk ahead of them as if they were not even there. This is not only an issue of etiquette and manners; it is also a matter of disrespect. The odds of another date, or even a friendship, will decrease significantly if you disrespect her by walking ahead of her and making it appear that she is less of a person than you.

Walk her to the door at the end of the date – Do not just reach across and open the car door from the inside and say good-night when you are taking a woman home. Get out of the car, walk around and open her door, and walk her to the house. Wait until she is inside, so you know she is safe, before returning to your car. If she insists that you not walk her to the door, you should still wait by the car until you see she is safely inside her house. Once again, show that she is worth the effort. Even if she does not say anything, you can be sure that she noticed your actions.

Turn off your phone – If you are on a date, TURN OFF YOUR PHONE. Do not even leave it on vibrate so that you are tempted to answer it if someone calls or texts. If you are out with a friend, it is okay to leave it on, but don't pay more attention to your phone than your company. You made a conscious decision to spend the day or evening with your date, so act like you want to be with her. There are obvious exceptions to this: if you are on call for a job or have a babysitter watching your children, etc., you should make that clear right up front so she does not feel that you are monitoring the phone for other reasons and disrespecting her.

There is nothing worse than spending time on the phone instead of with the person you are sitting with and supposed to be paying attention to.

Watch your language – You are not with "the guys," so watch your language, even if you are with someone you have heard use inappropriate language herself. It does not excuse you for doing the same. The same goes with jokes and stories: keep them clean. You can still be interesting and share some laughs without being vulgar. Show her the side of you that shows you are a "keeper," rather than someone she might spend some time with once in a while. Remember, one inappropriate comment could be the difference between establishing a long-term relationship or becoming a casual friend.

Conversation – Don't monopolize the conversation and talk about you and your thoughts the entire evening. Prior to the date, if at all possible, learn more about her likes/dislikes and steer the conversation in that direction. It will help keep the conversation flowing and you will get high marks for being a good listener and not just a bore. You can always add something about yourself in the event of one of those awkward silences. Just listening and allowing your date to share her thoughts, and showing interest, can make for a very successful evening. If you impress her on the first date, there will be more to follow and many opportunities to talk about yourself. Do not talk about past relationships. This could be the subject of conversations later in the relationship, but is not something you want to discuss on a first date.

Hygiene – Remember, you are on a date. You obviously wanted to go out with her, since you asked, so clean yourself up and dress appropriately. Wash your hair, clean your fingernails, brush your teeth, shower, etc.

Offering seats on public transportation – A gentleman should always offer his seat to a lady on public transportation such as a bus or train. There are exceptions to this, such as your health issues, or even the distance to be traveled, but as a rule, offer a seat. I think, in most instances, the seat will be refused. In my experience, more often than not, a younger woman might very well turn down the offer, especially if she is travelling just a short distance, but someone a little older might welcome the seat, regardless of the distance she is traveling.

Punctuality – Be on time. If you tell someone that you will pick them up at a certain time, then plan on leaving a little early, in case there is heavy traffic, etc. This is especially true if you are meeting at an outdoor area and not the safety and comfort of her own home. It is assumed that you've known of the date for at least a week, so planning should not be an issue. If for some reason you are going to be late, then call and let her know. Don't just leave her waiting because you will only be ten or fifteen minutes late. She will be wondering the entire time whether you are coming or if there was a problem or a change of plan. Take the time to let her know you will be late and when she can expect you to pick her up.

Offer jacket/sweater – It is often colder than expected in some restaurants, movie theaters, and other venues, so if you see your date is cold, offer your jacket. If you are aware that the place you are going is cold, let her know prior to the date. Either way, if you see she is cold, offer your coat.

Bad weather – In the event of bad weather, be sure to drop your date off at the entrance of the venue that you are visiting. When it is time to leave, bring the car around so she can stay dry.

Sending flowers – Make sure you do your due diligence before sending flowers. You don't have to come right out and tell someone you are going to send flowers, but during a conversation, ask the question about what kind of flowers she likes. This will let you know her preference in flowers, but also if she is allergic to any. Also ask her favorite color; maybe it will help you select a bouquet she will like. Remember, there are other flowers besides roses.

High heels – If the woman you are with is wearing high heels, do not walk over gravel or even grass. Stay on flat surfaces that allow her to walk in a normal manner and do not create a situation where she could fall and embarrass herself, or worse, hurt herself. Even if you have to walk a little further and it is inconvenient for you, suck it up and take care of her. She will appreciate your gesture.

SUMMARY: Obviously, not all of these examples apply in every situation, but most of them apply on dates and some apply when out with a female friend or coworker. The best way to learn is through practice. Also, when in doubt, do it. You can never go wrong by using good manners, with any woman, regardless of the situation.

3.

DATING ETIQUETTE

Etiquette: The formal manners and rules that are followed in social settings.

First Date

WHEN I FIRST STARTED DATING, I was nineteen years old. I remember it was right after I bought my first car. I was very awkward and shy as a young man and really had no idea what I was getting into. I did not have a father figure around to provide me with advice on the dos and don'ts when going out with women, or to let me know how I could get a woman's attention, and, most importantly, how to treat her while on a date. So all I could count on was what I heard from my friends who were already dating and what I had seen on television. When I was young, I enjoyed watching the old black-and-white movies that showed how men used to treat a woman like a lady.

I remember my first date vividly. I asked a girl out whom I had been interested in for a long time but never had the courage to ask out. For days prior to the date, I spent hours going over in my mind the things I should do and how I should behave in order to make a good first impression. I realized that the success of the first date not only dictated whether there would be future dates, but also how I would be judged by her friends as well, since she would undoubtedly be filling them in on the details of the date. My future dating life could be based on this one date. When I picked my date up at her house, I walked to the front door to meet her. When we walked to my car, I walked around to the other side of the car and opened the door for her. She actually seemed surprised that I opened the door, but thanked me and stated, "Bonus points for you." That registered with me. Throughout the date, which was dinner and a movie, I did those little things that I had seen on television or heard were the way to treat a lady. When we arrived at the restaurant, I quickly got out of the car and opened her door. I opened the door of the restaurant, allowing her to enter first. As we arrived at our table, I helped take off her coat and pulled out her chair. Each gesture earned me a smile and increased my confidence. At the end of the evening, I walked her to the door, and as she started to go into her house, she turned to me and thanked me for the evening and for treating her like a lady, and said that she looked forward to going out again. As I drove home, I thought about the evening and realized that what I had seen in those movies appeared to make a difference, and her smiles and comments directed toward those little things I did for her appeared to open the door for more dates.

Now, as I think back to her smiles and nods of approval, which made it obvious that being courteous and kind was appreciated, I have to wonder: Why is the art of being a gentleman disappearing? Why is what used to be common courtesy and a show of endearment becoming a thing of the past? Fortunately, you still see proper etiquette from men over a certain age, but what I see on a daily basis is that the younger generation no longer sees or feels the need to treat a woman in such a way. In the case of someone who does not have as much money as others, it could be these small gestures that make the difference between getting a second date, and potentially winning the heart of a woman, and not getting a second date. Just like in sports, everyone is looking for a competitive edge, and in the case of winning a woman's heart, simply being a gentleman could be the difference between a single date and a long-term relationship. I was a very average guy from a poor family, so I had to use every advantage I could find.

As my social life continued, I began watching couples and noticing how the men treated their dates. What I noticed fairly quickly was that the women with men who were chivalrous and gave them special attention seemed much happier and paid more attention to the men in return. The man who took off his partner's coat or pulled out her chair inevitably received a smile and sometimes a touch, showing appreciation for his act. They also appeared to have a friendlier and more open conversation. But the couples who came in with the man showing a lack of special treatment for his partner engaged in less interaction at the table.

Another thing I noticed was that in many cases, the men who treated women with courtesy and respect were generally with women younger than themselves. It made me wonder if the reason some women dated older men was that they were treated better by older men than they were by men their own age. While writing this book, I asked this question to many of the women I interviewed and was told by many of them that they preferred dating an older man or having a serious relationship with an older man because they treated women better and were not embarrassed to show them proper etiquette.

As I continued to keep my eyes open and pay attention to those things that a man would do for his date, I started keeping a list. I mean, I knew the basics, pulling out chairs, opening doors, etc., but there were things that men did that I had never thought of, and, in some cases, was not sure of the significance of and had to ask people or even use Google to find the answer.

Below are some useful guidelines that all men should consider:
When possible, ask a woman out at least one week in advance. Give her time to prepare for the date; maybe she wants to go out and buy something new to wear, or have time to change some plans. Last-minute planning will not favor you. Spontaneity is fine for future dates, but plan out the first date so you can increase your chances of success. Sometimes you want to surprise your date as to where you are taking her, but at least let her know what she should wear so you are both dressed appropriately. If the first date goes well, you will have opportunities to be spontaneous.

For the first date, ask her out in person; try not to do it over the phone and definitely do not text. If you care enough for the individual to ask her out and spend time with her, show her that you have enough confidence to ask her out face to face and can handle yourself in a social situation. Also, since it is the first date and you are not sure of how the chemistry will be, do not do something that will lock you together for a long period of time, just in case the two of you are ready to part company in a matter of an hour or even minutes. Another thing to think about is where the first date should be. Your best bet is a lunch or a dinner, nothing to follow. If the date is going well, you can always invite her for drinks to make the evening last longer. Also make sure it is a place that is not too loud to have a conversation. You do not want a loud club or a movie on your first date, or four hours later, you will say good-night and realize you still know nothing about each other.

Make sure you make a reservation when going to a restaurant. Show her that you are organized and care enough to make a plan rather than just hope for the best. This is your chance to make a good first impression.

Make sure you have enough money for the date and a credit card as backup. You never know if you'll have such a good time that you'll want to continue the evening and go somewhere after the original plans. If you asked her on the date, do not accept her offer to pay for her meal. You asked, you pay. On the occasion that she invited you, it is nice to make the offer and still pay, but you are off the hook if you do not have the funds.

After the date, when you are on your way home or when you are dropping her off, let her know that you had a good time and that you are interested in seeing her again. Take the lead in the relationship; you don't need to give the impression you want her to chase you.

Waiting three days to call someone you like is a myth. If you like her and had a good time on a date, let her know that night and give her a call sometime in the next day or two. There is a difference between letting someone know that you are interested and giving the appearance of a stalker. Call the next day or the second day; you will learn soon enough if your interest is shared.

Pay attention to basic etiquette; use proper table manners, such as keeping your elbows off the table and chewing your food with your mouth closed. Nothing can ruin a good meal quicker than sitting across from someone chewing or talking with a mouth full of food. If you are going fine dining, maybe you should find out what the different forks and spoons are for. Remove your hat as you enter the building. Once you pull out her chair and are seated, you could go all out and stand up anytime she leaves the table or returns. This is not practiced as widely as other etiquette, but it is a sign of being a gentleman.

If you are a sports enthusiast, do not go to a sports bar on the first date unless it is specifically to watch a game that she is interested in as well. Nothing is worse than trying to have a conversation with someone while they are obviously interested in something else, such as a sporting event. Once you get to know one another, it is not necessarily an issue on future dates, but the first date is your opportunity to impress her in other ways, not just with your sports knowledge. There are certain taboos for the conversation on the first date. First and foremost is that you don't talk about other women you have dated or bad experiences you have had with women. Also do not get too personal with your questions. This is a first date. It is used to get to know one another, but is not the time to try and learn every intimate secret about her. Many people do not like to share too much on the first date, so take your time and ask general questions that allow you to get to know her and allow her to see that you are an interesting, intelligent, and, most of all, normal guy.

Beyond the First Date

Now you have made it through the first date. Do not believe your friends when they tell you about the three-day rule. If the two of you had a good time, why confuse her or make her wonder about the success of the evening just because of a "Man Rule"? If you enjoyed yourself and are interested in seeing her again, give her a call and let her know. You do not have to ask her out immediately. However, there is nothing wrong with calling her the next day and letting her know you had a good time. I have heard all of the comments from men who say that we should wait until we hear from her, because calling first will give her the upper hand, etc. Well, based on my conversations, most women want to know if you had a good time as well. As I mentioned earlier, you do not have to call her the next day and ask her out again, but you can certainly call and let her know you had a good time. You should be able to tell from her reaction to your call if she is interested or not.

If, the following day, you call and thank her for the date and follow that with a simple question such as "What are you up to?" and she jumps right in and starts talking to you with no hesitation, then the odds are that the door is open and she is still interested in getting to know you. She is basically telling you that you did not screw up last night and she is open to continue getting to know one another. Now, there is no need to wear your heart on your sleeve and tell her how badly you are smitten with her; you don't want to scare her off. Talk for a bit and then, before she can say good-bye, do it yourself. Let her know that you enjoyed talking to her and that she should feel free to call you anytime. If the stars align and all is well with the world, you will receive a text sometime that day, just saying hello or asking how you are doing. If that happens, she has just let you know that you are welcome to ask her out on another date, so think about your next plan. That said, don't expect her to make the first contact after the date. Even if she likes you, she will most likely wait for the man to make the initial contact, but if she enjoyed herself as well, she will reply.

Hopefully, during the first date, which was probably a short lunch or dinner, you were able to talk and learn more about one another so the next date opens a few doors for your questions and insight about one another. In the event of a second date, I recommend staying away from just a movie, but you can certainly have dinner and then head to a good movie, especially if there is something playing that you know she wants to see. This is also your opportunity to start impressing her with your prowess in something you are good at, such as dancing. If you are good on the dance floor or maybe an above-average karaoke singer, you might want to lean in that direction. This is only the second date, so it is still all about her, but also your chance to impress her. It is still not necessary to be spontaneous at this point, so when you ask her out, if you are uncertain of what you would like to do, ask her. Yes, it is true that women, in general, like a man who can take charge and is confident, but you can certainly see if there is something she would like to do. If she says it is up to you, then take charge and tell her the plan. Do not appear indecisive. Tell her the plan and go.

4.

The Ladies Have Spoken (20s and 30s)

Courtesy: A respectful or considerate act or expression. Polite behavior.

While writing this book, I spoke with many women of different ages about their influences as they were growing up, their experiences with men as they began dating, and their expectations and thoughts now that they have some experiences under their belt. Originally, I was just going to have one chapter with comments from women of different ages, but because so many of the women I was interviewing wanted to put in their thoughts and experiences, I had to expand it to two separate chapters based on age. I broke the responses down into different age ranges, so that you might be able to see the differences in thoughts based on their ages and societal expectations during the periods of time that they were growing up. It also gave me a chance to discuss "then and now" with the older women. The next three chapters are the actual thoughts and comments from men and women I interviewed and are not my own words. I listed the state in which they grew up and their age. I informed them they could write as little or as much as they desired. There was no influence on the information they provided.

California, 20 – I agree that gentlemen have disappeared from our society. It is no longer expected that a man be inherently polite to anyone. I believe this change has taken place for a number of reasons. First and foremost, young men today believe this way of thinking is antiquated and unnecessary. The simple concept of "treat others as you would like to be treated" is no longer reinforced, and this causes people who are inherently self-centered to neglect the courtesies that we once considered commonplace. My male, and sometimes female, friends have made fun of me for adhering to such old-fashioned practices, and say that being nice and polite to women is a sign of weakness. I disagree. I consider it a sign of strength, because only a strong man can go against the normally expected practice, which unfortunately today is to show no chivalrous behavior toward women.

Virginia, 22 – The concept of the traditional "gentleman" brings up some really interesting thoughts and feelings for me. Growing up, like almost every little girl, I thought that one day when I was big and grown, I would meet my Prince Charming. He would be handsome, kind, and treat me like the princess I thought I was, and that simply would be my happy ending. Now that I am a little older, I realize that, as romantic as that fairy tale image may have seemed, I don't want any part of that dream to become a reality. I have had the opportunity to grow up in a generation where the roles of males and females in relationships have changed drastically. No longer are the days that it's expected to be married, have kids, and be a stay-at-home mother by the age of twenty-five. Gone are the days when women were expected to serve their husbands. I grew up in a generation where women were considered more as equals to their partners. I grew up in a generation where there are stay-at-home dads. I grew up in a generation where there are more women working and raising children alone than ever before. All this may be wonderful for the advancement of women in our society, but it brings its own challenges.

I believe that young women have become very sensitive to any type of behavior that may seem demeaning to women. For instance, if a man insists on ordering for a woman, or insists on paying for a meal, it's very possible that it could be taken as an insult rather than as an expected "gentlemanly" behavior. I don't want to defend all men and say they aren't at fault for treating women with the same respect as they used to, because they are somewhat at fault, but I do think that we, as a new generation of women, have created a confusing situation for many men. I personally feel that I am a very independent young woman. I am twenty-two, have a four-year college degree, a full-time job, and can successfully support myself independently. I love the fact that I can say I have worked to get where I am and that I like standing on my own two feet. I would never want to be the princess on a pedestal or be a housewife completely dependent on my husband. With that said, I still consider it an expectation for a man to hold the door open for me, offer me his jacket when I'm cold, and order for me in a restaurant. I understand how that can send mixed signals to men, which makes this traditional idea of the "gentleman" a little harder to maintain.

I think that it's very sad that it's not necessarily as common of a practice to show gentlemanly etiquette anymore, but it's not completely gone. There are still plenty of men, even my age, who hold true to those moral values and treat women with respect. I think the biggest difference now is that it's falling more on the women to hold men up to those standards. If we're going to change our role in the world and become more independent and take more control over our lives, then the same applies here. If you have expectations of a man you're dating, let him know up front what your expectations are so they are clear from the beginning. We're not in the position where we can wait passively for Prince Charming; we have to go out and get him.

Pennsylvania, 24 – As I was growing up, proper etiquette was the normal type of behavior in my home, an influence that actually became a burden to men as I grew into a young woman and began dating. As a child, my dad was always chivalrous with my mother, so it was the norm for me. When going out as a family, my mother and I would get into the car with assistance from my dad, walk into the restaurant with doors opened for us, and I wouldn't even have to touch the back of my chair. It was almost like a tradition. As I grew older, I realized that not everyone treated women that way. I was introduced to a different type of environment, one in which young men my age did not treat women the same way. When my parents split up, I moved with my mom to the

United States and experienced this new culture as I began to have a social life. It became so obvious to me that there was something lacking when it came to the behavior of the young boys my age. I discovered the new norm, the lack of politeness, the lack of respect, and the lack of caring about others' feelings. It was all new to me, very different than what I grew up with. When I started dating, I was not only opening my own door, but once in a while

I would look back to find my date texting on his phone. It appeared he had no clue that a simple gesture like walking beside me could have left a good impression; it was an opportunity lost. It did not take long for me to figure out that I would have to settle for less than I expected and what I believed I deserved. Fortunately, as I grew older and my social circle became larger, I found that there were some young men who still treated a lady in the way that I had become accustomed to at home while I was growing up.

My father came to see me as often as possible, and even as the years went by and we both grew older, he continued to treat me as a young lady, always doing those same things he did for my mother and me as when I was young. I realized that times were changing and you saw less and less of this kind of man. I was always so proud when we went out and he would open doors for me and pull out my chair, or help me with my coat. It was obvious that it was second nature for him and he did not even have to think twice about it. Being with him gave me hope that there must be some gentlemen out there. I have often seen older men treating their wives or dates in the same fashion, but I continued to hold out hope that I would find some men my age who still showed chivalrous behavior toward women. I was fortunate to date a few very nice young men, who were very nice and polite, and I was very sure to voice my appreciation and let them know how much I appreciated them being a gentleman. Fortunately, of the few college men that I met who really knew how to treat a lady and knew and understood proper etiquette, I was able to keep one for myself. I am lucky to have found a good man, who treats me the way my father treated my mother and me, and meets my earlier expectations in every way. I am happy to say that he is not someone who just treats women with respect until he gets what he is after. We have been together for a few years now, and he treats me the same way today as he did when we first met. I strongly believe had I not been surrounded by a man like my father as I was growing up, I would not have known what to look for in a man, and would have had no expectations, which is unfortunately the way many women are today. I am so happy my father taught me how men should treat women, because one thing is for sure, I will make sure my children will be taught the same things, so they can grow up respecting women and themselves and have high expectations from their prospective partners. I only hope that there are still men like that left so my children can find the same happiness that I have.

Florida, 25 – I grew up always being one of the boys. Getting dirty, running around with them, and even advising them on which women they should date or stay away from.

I didn't realize, until I got into my college, how rudely and disrespectfully men can treat women. Although there is a lack of true gentlemen in our American culture today, I do believe women have to take some of the blame for allowing it to happen. I feel that if you demand respect and hold yourself to a higher standard, men will follow suit even if they have shown, up to that point, they have no knowledge or experience of how to treat a woman. I have attended parties where there wasn't a gentleman to be found, but unfortunately, the woman accepted their behavior, rather than correcting it. I was right there at the party but held my ground, and men who wanted to talk to me had no choice but to treat me the way I expected to be treated. I was always one of a select few women who were not disrespected, because I would not allow it. Men offered me seats and drinks and spoke to me kindly. They made sure I was comfortable and never tried to make any inappropriate gestures. I couldn't help but notice that most women were not being treated the same way, because they did not demand to be treated with respect – they had no expectations.

What it comes down to is men will treat women the way we allow them to treat us. If women constantly allow men to talk down to them and not show some form of basic etiquette, such as opening doors and walking on the outside of a sidewalk, how can we expect the next generation to be any better? I don't want to come across as if I'm only blaming women for the way men treat them, because it appears that young men today do not even know basic etiquette, or even simple manners needed in social situations. However, society has changed, and women demand equality and ask less from men, so they can be seen and treated as equals, but then complain and get upset that men do not treat them as ladies. I challenge women to raise their standards and demand men treat them with the dignity and respect they deserve and should expect.

Hawaii, 33 – I am a woman born in the '80s. At that time, most males were not being taught the "old school" ways of treating a female. Many of the mannerisms taught to males when dating and being in a relationship with a woman didn't include opening doors, pulling out chairs, helping a woman with her bags, etc. Once I began dating, I didn't expect those things from the men I spent time with. This was not because it wasn't nice to receive this nice treatment from men, but because it wasn't something I had seen from men in the past, so I was not expecting it to be done for me. I had seen men treating women this way, but because it was something that was done before my generation, I only expected to see it in older men or on television. I've dated men who are my age and older. Most of them didn't exhibit this kind of behavior toward me or other women. These men weren't disrespectful or trying to make the point that women can do these things for themselves, so men shouldn't have to. They just haven't been taught the basics of chivalrous behavior.

Now, I understand that there are women who think that they can do things for themselves and don't need to be shown this level of courtesy from a man, but that doesn't mean that this chivalrous behavior would not be appreciated by those same women. Being an independent woman doesn't mean that we don't want to be treated special by a gentleman. It shouldn't be considered "special treatment" to want to have your door held open for you or your chair pulled out for you when eating at a restaurant. Of all the men I've dated, I have probably been shown this kind of treatment by two men. I have been dating for seventeen years! It felt so unnatural to have a man behave like a gentleman around me that I had to stop myself from automatically doing things that he wanted to do for me, like opening my own door or pulling out and sitting in my own chair. I think that women deserve to experience this kind of behavior. I don't feel it is meant to make a woman feel less about herself or like she can't do these things on her own. I don't feel these actions are used to take any power away from her as a woman of the twenty-first century. It is simply a man showing that he has enough care and respect for her as a woman to want to show her the most basic of considerations. It is quite refreshing in this day and age.

California, 37 – I have had the opportunity to go out with a number of gentlemen over the years and love being treated special and with respect. Fortunately, I did marry one of my gentleman suitors, and he contin- ues to treat me as a lady. I also had a few experiences with men who obviously did not grow up around well-mannered people and therefore did not know proper etiquette and how to treat a woman, on a date, or even in general. There have been a number of men who did not even do the basics like pulling out my chair or helping with my jacket; sad to say, there were a few who literally had no clue. They walked at least one step in front of me, opened the door and walked in before me, and just sat down at the table without offering to pull out my chair or even acknowledging me. In some cases, they were very financially well-off; it just appeared that they did not have a mentor when they were growing up to show them how to treat a lady. I would never go out on a second date with someone who did not know how to treat a lady. I was fortunate enough to meet some nice guys and, eventually, the perfect guy, who did then and still treats me special at every opportunity. As I look around now, I see less and less chivalry, and more couples who appear to be friends, even though they are on a date. I am not sure what it would take to reverse the current trend, but I would hope that someday, if I have a daughter, she will find a man who does know proper etiquette and gives her the special treatment that I think most women enjoy.

Okinawa, 38 – It seems that there aren't many gentlemen left in this world, but that quality is a requirement for someone I am considering dating. I am a very special woman, so why would I want someone who treats me differently?

The definition of a gentleman goes beyond the usual opening a door or pulling out my chair. Being a gentleman is being the ultimate man— taking out the trash, fixing a broken faucet, always pumping the gas, handling the tasks of putting together items purchased, carrying in the groceries, etc., without having to be asked. There is nothing sexier than a man who sees an issue and then handles the situation without asking.

Tenderness and patience are also traits of a true gentleman. I met a man long ago and it was two years before we kissed for the first time. We formed a true friendship before ever taking it to any other level. His kindness, patience, and overall gentlemanly nature endeared him to me. When we talked, he sought my opinion and genuinely cared about what I had to say. I always felt respected, cared for, and safe to express myself. Men like this don't come along very often and I was a very special woman to have gotten to experience this type of treatment. That said, I hope that this book reaches men everywhere around the world, as it is truly needed. Women value and deserve a true gentleman.

5.

The Ladies Have Spoken (40s and Over)

Social skills: The skills that are necessary to communicate and interact with others.

Las Vegas, 44 – My father was a gentleman. My best memory is from when I was seven years old. He brought me to my first fine-dining experience and treated me like a "little lady," pulling out my chair, ordering for me, teaching me proper table etiquette, and how a lady should act in different situations. Every day, my sisters and I witnessed to how my father treated my mother, with gentleness and respect. Even when they were mad at one another, he would still help her up the steps, or make sure she never carried anything heavy. My sisters and I grew up knowing and experiencing this. It was kind of a rude awakening when I started to date and realized that this is not true with all men. I particularly noticed that the younger the men were, the more clueless they were of gentlemanly manners. It seems that chivalry has to be ingrained in men during their upbringing, because it appears they won't learn it from other men because there appear to be very few role models when it comes to the proper way to treat women.

With all the gender-equality issues through the generations, I still believe deep down every woman would love to be treated like a lady. I for one was brought up by a strong-willed mother who insisted I become an independent, self-assured, confident woman who will never rely on any man for anything. But a simple gentlemanly act or gesture still melts my heart. It scores extra points for him as I find it so charming, and I will not hesitate or think twice about going out again with that particular gentleman.

I am fortunate in that the two significant men in my life are both gentlemen. But there are still times when I wish they'd let their guard down and relax a bit. Being proper in public is wonderful, but there are moments when you just want to say, "Hey, I truly appreciate the way you're treating me, but can you just kiss me already?" I guess I'm one of the lucky ones. Because of the environment and culture I grew up with, my expectations are high, but it doesn't necessarily mean I always have to be treated special. Worrying about how other people think is manly and shows the real nature of a gentleman in my definition.

South Carolina, 46 – When I was growing up, the repetitive message in my household was, "Don't depend on any man. Get an education and have your own career." This was because my mother felt trapped by the expectations of the society she grew up in. She married and started a family too young and did not want that for me. This message was resounding and prevalent amongst the mothers of my generation, and served as the foundation for the confusion I think a lot of women my age faced in young adulthood.

What does independence mean? Some took this as a message that marriage and family was a trap that would bind you in domestic servitude. Others looked at this as a reason to thwart chivalrous acts by men since they spoke to an idea that women could not take care of themselves. My take was a bit more objective. Chivalry was originally reserved for women of high standing in the community. His actions conveyed respect, care, and concern for these women. The intent of the actions was not to make a woman feel less important; it was to demonstrate the opposite. Who wouldn't want to feel that way?

During my dating years, the boys who stood out were those that adhered to the expectations of polite society. They made me feel the most respected and considered. Their actions demonstrated that they cared about me. The first date with the man I would marry was by far the most noteworthy. He opened the car door for me, he asked what I wanted to listen to on the radio, he opened doors, pulled out chairs, and even ordered for me at the restaurant. While his nerves showed in many of his actions, this too was endearing.

We have been married for many years, and he is still doing things like this for me. I don't perceive any of these actions as demeaning because I understand both the intent and the message. He's not telling me that he respects, loves, and cares for me, he's showing me, and actions speak louder than words.

Japan, 47 – I was fortunate to have an opportunity to study abroad in the '80s. There were a few occasions that I went to the school parties with groups of friends. Because they were casual parties, none of my male friends were expected to act in a gentlemanly manner, such as opening a car door or pulling out a chair. However, when I went to the prom, my male friend opened the car door for me and escorted me to the party. As Japan is a man-dominated country, we have no expectations of special treatment toward women. Based on the prom, I assumed those behaviors took place only for special/formal occasions and I didn't think much of it. What really impressed me was when I went out for dinner with a college boy one night. He dropped me off at my house and waited for me till I was safely inside of the house rather than quickly driving off to his home. My American exchange-student mother said the boy was well mannered, explaining to me that a gentleman should not leave until his date is safely inside the house. It was a bit of a culture shock at first, because I never felt danger walking on the streets alone late at night in Japan. However, the more I think of it, it is very nice and even important that men treat women in a certain manner.

I saw a very interesting Japanese TV show the other day. The TV crews were in Tokyo, interviewing ladies from various countries who are dating Japanese men, asking what they like and dislike about Japanese men. Several ladies pointed out Japanese men are not "gentlemen." I agree with their comment, but I must say, I don't see many American men now that I associate with acting as gentlemen either. From that night on, I started paying more attention to how American men act toward women. I once saw a young American couple at a restaurant who were also with two other male friends. She spoke to him while he was texting or busy doing something with his cell phone. Her approach must have been annoying to him. He yelled at her in front of their friends. She left the restaurant without a word. I simply thought "gentleman" means you do nice things for women like pulling out chairs or helping put coats on, but being respectful, especially in public, is very important. I would hope to see more men show respect toward women, and I believe this goes both ways; women also should show respect toward men.

Colorado, 48 – I was fortunate to spend my younger years surrounded by gentlemen. Sometimes I think it was the influence of living in a military community and other times I credit living in the South. But even in the '80s people were astounded by gentlemanly etiquette. Prior to my high school prom, my date took me to dinner at a restaurant on the beach. He came around and opened the car door for me and a crowd of tourists cheered for him. Little did they know that these actions were normal for him. I learned that, with him doing those nice, unspoken things for me, I wanted to do nice things for him in return – like baking his favorite dessert or serving him a glass of iced tea as soon as he came over to my house to spend time with me. I wanted to take care of him as he was taking care of me. I dated other men in my twenties and learned that not all men are gentlemen. I was so excited to have a date with a popular morning-show disc jockey. We went to a play together, and when we stopped at the coat check, he quickly took off his coat, handed it to the attendant, and walked away without helping me with my coat. I was floored and so disappointed that even though I don't remember the play, I have never forgotten that incident! A good friend of mine who I met many years ago was a perfect gentleman and was a huge influence on my future husband – he watched and emulated my friend until he won my heart. Even though our marriage ended in divorce, I still consider my ex a gentleman – who always opened doors, held out chairs at restaurants, helped me with my coat on and off, and scraped ice off of my car in the morning and made sure it was warmed up for me! And in return, I would make his favorite meals, starch his shirts, and prepare his tea or coffee in the morning even if it meant I had to wake up earlier to accommodate his schedule.

I've been divorced for five years now and have slowly made my way back into the dating pool. I'm surprised that a lot of men today don't possess gentleman qualities, but even more surprised by the men who have verbally tried to convince me that they are gentlemen without ever showing me any kind of gentlemanly etiquette. I was on a date with a man – we had taken two cars and decided to come back to my place. As we started driving, he drove behind me. I felt safe and it really warmed me up to him…until the road expanded with more than one lane and he took off in front of me like a bat out of hell. I couldn't believe it! As soon as we got to my place, I expressed my disappointment, and he looked at me like I was crazy. I gave him another chance – he did the same thing, but that time I never met him back at my place. I stopped at a coffee shop by myself to regroup. It took him almost forty-five minutes to realize that I hadn't reached my house, because he had been sitting in his car playing on his phone! I'm raising two boys to be men and I couldn't allow this man to influence them in any way. When I told him that I didn't want to date him anymore, he tried to convince me of what a great role model he was for my boys. It was very sad because he never paid attention to what I had told him. I haven't met anyone special yet, but I do have hope and I do believe that gentlemen still exist. And if there are men out there that aren't sure how to be a gentleman, I hope they're reading this book right now!

Alaska, 50 – I do appreciate a chair being pulled and a door being opened for me regardless of the mood I am in. However, let me start by prefacing that I am a selective feminist. I want to be treated as an equal in the boardroom and on the battlefield, be dominant outside the workplace, but still want doors opened and chairs pulled out for me. In the same vein, if I am the suitor, my expectation is that I am the one who exhibits the gentlemen qualities. I believe in social equality when it comes to dating practices, whether or not the date is a new acquaintance, significant other, boyfriend, or spouse.

So where did my thought process originate? It did not originate from watching my father and how he treated my mother. Rather, my thought process came from watching old black-and-white movies. I was attracted by the clothes, the way that individuals spoke to each other, and how men and women were treated, regardless of socioeconomic status. So, in retrospect, media was my learning tool. With today's technological advances we have lost those important tools for being able to communicate and behave more effectively – the art of conversation and face-to-face interactions. However, don't get it twisted. It is not completely the males' fault for the loss of gentlemen qualities. We women have had a prominent role in squelching gentlemen behaviors.

In the '60s and '70s, we asserted ourselves by burning bras and abandoning the notion of a traditional woman. In the '80s and '90s, we demanded equality on all levels in our professional as well as personal lives. No longer did we want to do all the housework while the men slayed the dragon and gathered the food. We wanted to slay the dragon alongside our male counterparts, while they, in turn, stood alongside us while doing the dishes, sorting the laundry, and rearing the children. In the process, we ridiculed and berated men for demonstrating gentlemen-like behavior because the behaviors were equated to downgrading the contribution of women in society. Gentlemanly behaviors were marked as indicators that women were to remain in a weak and submissive manner. In essence, we went from one extreme to the other. In today's world, I can see how it may be confusing for males to know when to engage in gentlemanly behavior and when to just let it go. So what do I do? My part, by letting my gentleman know my expectations.

Hawaii, 50 – Looking back on my dating experiences, I realized earlier than most women that I would never be in a relationship with a man who wasn't a gentleman. I was lucky enough to be loved by someone special, and I have him to thank and to measure all the men who followed against.

Dating younger men had its plusses and minuses. For starters, on the plus side, I found they were generally more fun and adventurous and able to keep up with me. However, eventually, their shortcomings of not knowing gentlemanly etiquette became an issue. They lacked the true understanding of the importance of simple manners, such as opening a door, pulling out a chair, or even sending flowers, those small things that make a woman feel special. Certainly some of them tried to treat me as I expected, and most women expect, but the effort was inconsistent and didn't appear natural, but rather forced. Eventually, I became frustrated with their lack of knowledge of proper etiquette and it led to problems and eventual breakups.

When I date men my age, I find their lack of proper etiquette even more disappointing than when I date younger men. I guess that since they grew up the same time I did, there was an expectation that they would be well aware of proper etiquette, but it appears that they never learned it, or were just not interested in treating a woman that way. This is not to say that all men my age behave this way, but it tends to be the norm. When I look at my generation, and prior generations, we all grew up with the same television shows, the same media outlets, hopefully the same good core values, but something happened and gentlemanly behavior, chivalry, proper etiquette, just somehow disappeared. But I do know that for me to be with a man, his being a gentleman is top priority.

Thank goodness for older men, because it seems they have not forgotten how to treat a lady. They learned how to do it right, and continue to do so. The older men I have spent time with knew how to make a woman feel good. They go out of their way to make a woman feel special, like the woman they are with is the only woman they are interested in. This treatment also makes them seem so confident in themselves, and happy that their companionship is desired.

It is obvious that through time, treating a woman as a lady has become a thing of the past, but I can't help but wonder why it is so difficult for a man to do simple things to make his partner happy, especially if it means special treatment from his partner in return.

Georgia, 52 – My father passed away when I was five years old and I never really got the chance to have a good male role model in my life. My mother would tell me many stories of the way my father treated her and what type of man he was. Through her stories I was able to formulate the type of man I wanted to marry, what I consider to be a real gentleman. My father was a great man of character who was always a bright spirit even in the darkest of times. My mother often said that there was never a time when she was upset that he didn't tell a corny joke, buy her favorite piece of candy, or bring home her favorite dessert. He made her feel like she was the only woman in the world; he nurtured her, encouraged her, and made her feel like a queen. My father was the gentleman I never met.

A true gentleman cannot be stereotyped. He appears in all shapes, ethnicities, economic backgrounds, etc. He doesn't just open doors or put on your coat. I once dated someone who did the minor niceties in the beginning, but it was not in the core of him. Anyone can open the door for you; anyone can pull out your chair; but the substance of a man shows eventually. Through the love of a true gentleman, you feel respected, beautiful, amazing…alive. You feel as if you could do anything, and that if you failed, he would still love you. He is open and honest with his feelings and never makes you doubt the love you share or your self-worth. You feel confident and secure in his love. My mother always told me that I would know within the first twenty-four to forty-eight hours if a man is for me. You don't have to wait a week, a month, or a year. If he is the one, it is obvious from the moment you spend time with him. The man that I ended up marrying was a true gentleman and we raised our sons to be the same. As parents, it is our job to plant that seed in our sons so that their gentleman spirit can carry on from generation to generation.

New York, 58 – Earlier this week, a sixty-four-year-old woman complained to me about the lack of gentlemanly manners among young men. According to her, three U.S. soldiers under the age of twenty-five saw her approach a closed door as she was carrying a small crate of books and her handbag. She said that neither one of the young men stood up and opened the door for her, nor did they assist her with the crate. She was outraged about their lack of manners. As we tried to figure out why they failed to assist her, she concluded that they just did not have good home training. I agreed with her.

I grew up in the United States in the '60s and '70s, when young male children and adolescent males were taught by their parents and other relatives certain behaviors that gentlemen should exhibit. Furthermore, at a very young age, I learned how a lady or young girl was to be treated by males. I acquired this knowledge mostly through observation of how my stepfather interacted with my three sisters and me. Even before we reached adolescence, he treated us as young ladies by holding the door open, helping us with our coat, and pulling our chair out at the table so that we could be seated. I can distinctly recall a time when my stepfather and I were walking down the street in NYC. I was closer to the curb than he was. He gently moved me to the inside of the sidewalk. That was a profound moment for me. I felt protected and valued as a result of my stepfather's actions.

Mama also taught my three younger brothers the importance of being a gentleman. Before they reached adolescence, Mama and Daddy had taught them to hold the door for females and give up their seat rather than have a lady stand. I would have to agree that gentlemanly behaviors are something that a young man should learn at home.

In my opinion, the lack of respect for women has become pervasive in America during the last twenty-five years. Men do not treat women as they did thirty years ago. The loss of certain courtesies in our society can be attributed to a number of factors, the main factor being the feminist movement; many women have adopted the attitude that "I don't need a man to do… I can do it just as good as a man." Since the 1960s the role of the American woman has changed. Thus, the dynamics between men and woman have changed.

Ohio, 58 – My observation of a true gentleman is a man who is comfortable with himself and who carries himself with a sense of pride and a high self-esteem. Men with these values have the ability to express themselves and include their significant other in encompassing these feelings as a relationship evolves. A true gentleman is considerate of the feelings of those that are close to him and consistently engages himself in knowing the things that are most important in a woman's life as well as his own. The open lines of communication build a trust that elevates the gentleman in everyone's eyes that observe him in his daily life and actions.

Alaska, 61 – I was raised by conservative parents and my father was most certainly a gentleman. I have two brothers and my dad was a strong role model for both of them. I dated my share of guys and was twenty-eight when I got married. My husband and I moved to Europe with his job not long after we got married and I feel that is where we both learned how to be married. There were not parents or friends to run to when the going got tough. We both had to learn the value of compromise and, fortunately, we did that. My husband was always a gentleman where I and others were concerned. But it took us both a while to learn to treat each other with the respect that I feel makes my marriage work today. We've had thirty-three great years together living in many different locations. We're nearing retirement and plan to spend a number of years traveling abroad. We get along great, we love being together, and I'm happy to say, my husband is a true gentleman. He frequently goes out of his way to do nice things for me and I often have other women express envy for the great marriage that we have. I believe that expressing myself to my husband as a caring person – doing the little things for him as he does for me – is what I need to do to allow him to be the gentleman that I want him to be.

Florida, 77 – My father was a hardworking man who took good care of his family, but I do not recall him ever doing those special little things, like pulling out her chair, or helping my mother with her coat, making sure her glass was full, or any other signs of etiquette, other than occasionally opening the door for her. Because of this, I really did not have expectations of my partner as I grew older and started to date. I ended up marrying one of the town's "bad boys," handsome, strong, active, everything a woman might look for in a man, except when it came to romance and being a gentleman; they were just not his strong suit. He joined the military very young, and most of the next twenty years we spent apart because of his Army career. I raised six kids, pretty much on my own, and by the time I was thirty, having someone pulling out a chair for me, or sending me flowers, was not something I had time to think about.

Things changed for me when I moved to my current home and saw how the majority of the men here treated their wives and female friends. Unfortunately, this was when I was already in my sixties. But it was nice to see men who actually took the time to show proper etiquette toward women. I guess the good thing is I have had the opportunity to enjoy being treated this way for a number of years now, so I know it exists and how nice it can make a woman feel. I see and experience it every day now. The average age of the men is seventy years old, but you can see that the majority of them have treated women this way for many years.

I can certainly say that if given a choice, I would definitely choose to be with a man who made an effort to treat me special and do those small things that make women feel good and showed he truly cared. I now know, after so many years, just how important this is. If I had the opportunity to provide any advice to young women, it would be to find a man that treats you like you are the woman he wants to be with. If he doesn't already do it, let him know your expectations, and if he is not willing to meet them, then he is probably not someone you want to waste a lot of time on. I am very happy that my daughter has found a man who treats her with nothing but dignity and respect and is a gentleman toward her at all times. I am so happy that she found this type of man at a young age.

I eat out at restaurants quite often and I can see the lack of chivalry among the younger men. I wish there was a way to reverse the trend and get men to start treating women like ladies again. Unfortunately, until women start asking or demanding it from their dates and partners, I can imagine things will only get worse and someday chivalry will be a thing of the past. Three cheers for the gentlemen who are still out there.

6.

MAN UP! WHAT ARE THEIR THOUGHTS?

Feminism: The advocacy of women rights on the grounds of political, social, and economic equality to men.

AFTER GIVING WOMEN THE OPPORTUNITY to voice their thoughts, I thought it only fair to hear from a few men. Though every man I talked to while writing this book agreed that men no longer treat woman as they did ten to twenty years ago, amazingly enough, they all placed the blame on the ladies. The majority of the men stated that women no longer want to be treated specially; they want to be equals, and therefore the men no longer even attempt to show any etiquette. The rest of the men simply said that women just don't care, and allow men to treat them poorly. That is their expectation, so that is how they get treated. As you read in the comments from the women, a few of them stated the same concern. It is nice to know that there are men out there that still treat their dates/partners with proper etiquette, and have no intention of stopping. Here are a few of the comments from some of the men I talked to:

California, 20 – I agree that the "gentleman" has disappeared from our society. It is no longer expected of a man to be inherently polite to anyone, and I believe this change has a variety of causes. The first and foremost is that young people, male and female, view chivalry and a generally polite nature as antiquated and unnecessary. The simple concept of "treat others as you would like to be treated" is no longer reinforced, and this causes people, who are inherently self-centered, to neglect the courtesies that were once considered "common." My male and, occasionally, female peers have made fun of me for adhering to such "old-fashioned" practices, and treat me as though going out of my way to be helpful and polite shows some kind of weakness. I believe another cause for this shift is the rise of the modern feminist. Several times when trying to be polite and chivalrous with my female friends, I have been treated with suspicion, and occasionally accused of misogyny. Simply holding a door open for a woman apparently warranted a claim that I "didn't think she could do it herself," even though I hold the door open for anyone immediately ahead of or behind me, regardless of gender. Reactions like this make me pause before trying to help someone, even though I believe it is right, and it makes me feel good about myself. Helping someone pick up change or carry a package can help make someone else's life easier, if only a little bit, and is therefore worth doing. It is truly regrettable that modern behavior has put so little emphasis on manners. Hopefully the "gentleman" can make a resurgence in our culture.

Colorado, 32 – I am not exactly sure where I learned how to be a "gentleman." I believe it was a mixture of things. The way my mother raised me probably had the biggest influence. Hanging out with different groups of people when I was younger, listening to different styles of music, watching different kinds of movies, and seeing how my friends treated women (each one a different way) were all contributing factors.

I see pop culture and parenting as the main reasons the way men treat women has changed so drastically. There just seems to be no courtesy toward other people, poor table manners are the norm, horrible grammar abounds, and yes, chivalry no longer exists. As mentioned above, while growing up, my friends who listened to only rap music and only watched movies such as *Friday, Boyz n the Hood, Menace II Society*, etc., regularly referred to girls with the same derogatory names they heard in the music they listened to and movies they watched. Then there was the other group of friends, the ones who, much like me, were more diverse in their music and movie selection. Along with rap and the movies mentioned above, we enjoyed other styles of music and movies such as country music and movies and a good comedy or "chick flick."

By being exposed to more options, I quickly learned what road I preferred when it came to treating women, and people in general. I spent a number of my younger years in Germany and still visit there on occasion. Germany is a country whose people are very well mannered and treat people with respect. When I come back to the U.S., the difference in the way people treat one another never ceases to amaze me. I think the way we treat others goes back to parenting. For example, I just recently took a trip to Germany for Christmas. On the flight, a little German girl, no older than five, was asking her father countless questions about the airplane. He was the perfect parent in my eyes, as he answered every question, remained patient, joked, and laughed with his little daughter. Two weeks later, back in the U.S., I was in a store and ran into a similar scenario. A little girl, no older than five, was asking her mom many questions. I don't recall the subject of the questions, but I do recall how her mother responded, and could not believe my ears. Her mother said something along the lines of, "You ask too many God d——n questions! Shut up and keep f——kin' walking." Enough said. Another example happened just the other day. I was sitting in my car, in a parking lot. Next to me was a male with his daughter in the backseat. They were apparently waiting for someone. Once again, she couldn't have been a day older than five. He was listening to and singing along to rap songs, in which I heard very rude words for men and women's body parts. What kind of expectations will she have as she gets older on how men should treat her?

Nowadays, girls as young as thirteen are out on the dance floor partying and celebrating to lyrics and names for women that insult and denigrate them, and they are loving it. What does that say about them, their upbringing, and future expectations? As sad as it is to say, there is no hope for change for a big part of the population, because this generation will raise their children just as they have been raised. Maybe it would help if a huge nationwide campaign would be started.

Sometimes I wonder how men who treat and talk to women in such a vulgar way attract women at all. I'm guessing those girls/women just do not know any better because it is how they were raised and they were never exposed to anything better. I'm just glad to know there is still a small percentage of men and women who know what is right. Thanks to them, we will continue to have a small minority of men who know how to treat women, and who knows, maybe someday it will catch on and people will start treating people with dignity and respect once again.

Washington, 44 – First, I want to define what chivalry means to me since it's not a word commonly used in today's vernacular. Today, simply stated, chivalry equates to three things that can be espoused by both men and women. To be or to exhibit chivalrous (gentlemanly) behavior means to:

1. Set a good example and demonstrate respect in a relationship. *Treat others as you want to be treated.*

2. Consistently display a life of courtesy and good character. *Be faithful.*

3. Live a principled and well-mannered life. *Contribute to society.*

Living a chivalrous life is a choice that all men and women can demonstrate. It's a choice to do the right thing all the time for the right reasons. It's about maintaining dignity and respect in a relationship or toward the opposite sex (or same sex for that matter).

When a man demonstrates chivalry towards a woman, it shows the woman that he respects her and cares for her; in other words, he treats her like a lady. And in return, hopefully, the lady loves and respects the man. In my opinion, chivalry goes beyond the shallow, old-fashioned interpretation of "holding doors open, helping with her coat, and pulling her chair out at dinner." It definitely includes these grand gestures, but is so much more all-encompassing. Being chivalrous today means respect goes both ways. If a woman doesn't live the same principles of being "chivalrous," then the relationship will never be successful. For the man who fails to live up to his responsibility as a male, then their relationship is doomed to fail. Get off your lazy ass and be responsible and make a person feel as if they are the most important person in the world and show some signs of affection. And in return, you will be appreciated and respected as well. Both men and women want to feel appreciated, loved, and cared for, because it feels good when you are respected.

Most don't realize they are exhibiting some form of chivalrous behavior when they keep the door open for someone, serve them a drink first, or, if they are married or dating, hold one's hand in public or in a movie, give your loved one a kiss at bedtime or in the morning before you depart for work, or simply just make the bed. In today's culture, even going as far as folding laundry or cleaning dishes is considered "today's chivalrous actions." You are demonstrating respect by sharing in responsibilities and not solely placing the onus on the female. Moreover, it's as simple as giving up a coat when it's cold outside or holding someone close to your body to keep them warm on a cold winter's day. It's about making coffee in the morning or preparing dinner in the evening. Sometimes it's the simple acts that can make the biggest difference.

Three primary reasons why men do not demonstrate chivalry:

1. Men are not raised to be chivalrous (but can learn through watching others and being mentored).

2. Men are lazy and don't care about treating women like they should be treated. Often times, it's about ME.

3. Men do not feel women want a person to be chivalrous (which is a completely wrong assessment).

The vicious cycle unfolds with the female, because they have lowered the standards and go along with any guy that shows them any level of attention. I have witnessed, like many of you have (some of you may have even experienced this), relationships where the female gives up easily with a guy who lacks in chivalry, and unfortunately, most of these relationships are short-term. Oftentimes these females settle to be in the relationship, and/or these females may not necessarily know what "chivalry" is because they have never witnessed it or experienced it. Likewise, it's a horrible excuse for those that say, "Women want to be treated as equals, and therefore, chivalry is dead." Chivalry is dead only if the person allows it to be dead. Everyone, both men and women, can be treated as "equals" while demonstrating chivalrous actions.

Furthermore, why is it that when we attend formal functions, i.e. a prom for teens or a formal ball for adults, we see acts of chivalry? Does it take a special occasion with everyone dressed up to demonstrate proper manners and respect toward our "partner?" Is it because we are "expected to do it" at these events? Is it because if we don't "perform," we will get ridiculed? Chivalry should not be a part-time characteristic...but rather a full-time trait inculcated in the person's mind. It's a principled way of life. A good indicator of the kind of life you are living and how you are projecting yourself to the world is to look at your kids. Are they treating everyone with respect (including you, the parent), using proper manners (yes, ma'am), voluntarily helping where they can (chores, helping a neighbor bring in groceries)? It doesn't always have to be some grandiose gesture, just the simple things that have been easily overlooked sometimes mean so much more.

For those of you who are reading this, you know what I am talking about. Are you to blame or are you blaming others? Let's not use the "I wasn't raised like that" excuse. Nor should we use the "their dad was never around...I am single-parenting" excuse. You have the opportunity to change it for your own kids today. My dad passed away when I was in middle school and I didn't get a good example of chivalry growing up most of my life, but I chose to learn and be chivalrous nonetheless. Whether single-parenting by choice or not, you have the option to decide how to lead your life and display to your kids the kind of life you want them to lead. My wife was holding a job and single-parenting for five years while I was deployed to Afghanistan and Iraq, yet she consistently demonstrated the importance of values, respect, responsibility, and principles. The choice to lead a chivalrous life is ultimately yours and yours alone.

I met my wife when we were in fifth grade, and we have been happily married for over twenty-one years. I attribute our successful marriage to the simple fact that we both love and respect each other and we actively apply the three principles identified earlier. I love her today more than ever before, and when we go on date night, it's like going out on a date for the first time. It's that special for us. We've had our challenges, but through the challenges, we have matured, grown, and learned from each other. After all, we did agree to our marriage as "unconditional." We are blessed to have two wonderful boys who have front-row seats to parents who love and respect each other and get to experience the lasting benefits of what it means to have a strong, vibrant, and loving family who contributes to society. Our boys in essence are growing up in a principled environment and, because of the time and effort we place in our marriage, they are learning how to be chivalrous in more ways than one.

So let's face it, we are no longer knights in shining armor, but that does not mean you can't exhibit today's chivalrous characteristics. It's a different world today, filled with technology, high-speed communication, and access to unlimited resources. If you are only equating chivalry with opening the doors and pulling out the seats, you are missing the point, which is often the case in many instances, as evidenced by today's divorce rate, where it is common to read that over 50% of marriages end in divorce. Chivalry means nothing unless you truly want to change and put forth the necessary effort to live a principled life.

Florida, 46 – Men are physically built the way we are to physically take care of our wives, our children, and our homes. That's the way God made us. Our job is to protect our families – with our lives if we have to. Women aren't helpless, but men should always be ready to keep them from harm or hardship, sacrificing ourselves if necessary. Families always come first; the men are second. Men don't hit or hurt girls, ever. That's pretty basic, but always worth restating. I don't care what happens; men don't abuse women. We don't raise our voice or yell, either. Trying to scare a girl is weak. Bad language, off-color jokes, and things like that aren't appropriate and not what a real man should do in front of a girl. For single guys (and married ones too), you don't "kiss and tell." Personal and intimate details are kept between a man and woman. It looks weak to share things with others that show your lady is anything less than a lady. It's not respectful or gentlemanly in my opinion.

My dad also taught me that women are to be honored and treated well always. In fact, the true test of a man is what he's willing to give up to protect a girl, take care of her, or provide her. I know as a father of both a son and a daughter, these lessons are very important for me to pass along to them too.

For background, my mom and dad were relatively conservative Southern parents. I was raised with a "no ma'am, no sir...yes ma'am, yes sir" kind of mentality. When I look back on it, everyone in my family – both the north Florida and the southern Georgia sides – were all raised the same. In fact, I remember that was pretty much the norm among all of my neighbors growing up. I never sensed that women didn't like that or found it offensive to be treated like a lady. Even today, despite the feminist push and what I would say are very destructive pop-cultural influences, I would argue that all women at heart want to be treated as ladies by a true gentleman.

Perhaps most importantly, though, as I write this, this is how I treat my daughter and raise my son. I know that the way I treat my daughter, my wife, and all women impacts my daughter's own sense of self-worth and expectations of a man. I want my daughter to see what a man should strive to be (to the best of my ability of course – I'm definitely far from perfect) so that she isn't misled and doesn't accept anything less when she starts dating. Same thing for my son. He needs to know early on what it means to protect and defend his sister. I drill that into him constantly. It starts there and continues with how he should treat girls that he meets later in life too.

Chivalry as a concept isn't dead, it just isn't practiced by enough men, I think – and there's no excuse not to. People shouldn't be misled by the way the media portrays men-women relationships. Instead, they should look at the way the Bible actually defines our roles, and it becomes very clear. Honor, protect, provide, and respect always. I'm admittedly old-fashioned in this regard. This is how I look at being a gentleman.

South Carolina, 47 – Being a "gentleman" goes way beyond proper etiquette and being polite. It is rooted in the cultural values that we grow up with. I was fortunate enough to have positive male (and female) role models, who demonstrated a certain type of social conduct, on whom I modeled my behavior. From an early age, I was taught to be respectful of my elders and of women. That may now sound old fashioned, but it is a timeless lesson that I still try to uphold. For example, I have been happily married for twenty-five years, and I am still good friends with every girlfriend that I had prior to my marriage. Why? I can only attribute it to the fact that I was honest and respectful to them during the entire relationship (to include the breakup), and that we took the time to communicate with one another. I can't speak for all men, but I will say that mutual respect goes a long way toward establishing an enduring friendship and partnership. A quick story: On one of the first dates with my future wife, I tried to serve her the fajitas that the waiter brought to the table. I was so nervous that I burnt my fingers on the tray. I am sure that there are many guys who would say that it's a perfect example why NOT to be a gentleman, but despite my short-term pain, my date was so impressed with my attempt that she accepted my next offer for a date. Twenty-five years and two kids later, we're still together.

Alabama, 54 – My parents are traditional Southern conservatives from northern Alabama. My father taught me how to treat women in general by his words and the example he set by how he treated my mother. I learned a great deal about how to treat women from my mother and all my female relatives. All the women in my family (both sides) are extremely strong women who command respect...without having to demand it. They all taught me that a lot was expected of me as a man, but nothing was more expected than that I grow up to be a good man who treated everyone with dignity and respect. And they all went out of their way to teach me HOW to show my respect for women.

As a man, I was expected to lead my wife and my family. And just as in the Army, leaders have to be selfless. This means always putting your wife and children first...in everything. Many of the chivalrous customs of how to show respect for my wife really are just selfless examples of putting your wife first and yourself second. Things like opening car doors, carrying anything heavy so she doesn't have to, giving her my coat if she's cold, allowing her to have the one open seat on the bus or subway, all of these are simply ways of showing respect for your spouse.

This same philosophy transcended the family. A good man treats everyone with dignity and respect, and the way you showed dignity and respect for all women was the same way you showed it for your wife: you put them first. As I mentioned, all the women in my family were extremely strong. They were also fiercely loyal and devoted to their husbands, but make no mistake about it, they chose their husbands, not the other way around. And not a single one of them would have chosen a man to be their husband who didn't put them first and treat them with absolute respect. All the women in my family constantly reinforced this message. They reinforced it by the things they taught me, by their conversations with one another, and by their actions. Can't tell you the number of times I've heard women in my family point out times they saw men doing the right thing or not doing the right thing in the way they treated women. So much so that these traits were ingrained in me. They were also ingrained in my sister and the other younger women in my family. None of them would give a man that didn't treat them with absolute respect a second thought. I believe most women still want to be treated with respect in the same manner, but not all. I always find it funny when a woman reacts negatively when I hold a door open for her but this seldom happens. And when it does, I don't let it deter me; the vast majority of women still appreciate this.

Florida, 54 – I grew up in a pretty typical traditional family. My parents were respectful of one another for the most part. My parents did not focus on how to treat a woman but taught us to be respectful and kind to all people regardless of race, sex, creed, or color. They taught us that everyone, regardless of their title or financial status, was worthy of kindness and equal time.

In addition there was always a great emphasis on the importance of family. Therefore it makes sense to me that if you are taught to be a kind, respectful person to strangers then it's even more important to treat your family, wife, and children that way. As an adult, I figured out that, like a relationship or investing in real estate or weight lifting, there are no shortcuts or magic formulas, just hard work and commitment. I am a firm believer that you get out what you put into a relationship. Today the overall relationship between men and women has culturally changed. The world is a much more level playing field with both sexes taking equal roles in all aspects of personal and business life. So I believe that men view women as equals, therefore finding chivalry outdated and possibly unwanted.

California, 55 – I do not recall a woman ever telling me "no" when I offered to open a door for her, nor do I recall a woman that I was on a date with refusing my offer to pull out her chair. I realize that times and expectations have changed, but I like bringing a smile to a woman's face with a simple gesture or act of kindness. Personally, I don't think that it has to only be with a date. To me, a gentleman treats everyone with dignity and respect, regardless of age or social status, or if they are on a date with me or just someone walking down the street that I see could use some help carrying a package, opening his/her trunk, or holding something while they look for their keys or put a child in the car. There are things that we as men can do every day to make someone feel good and bring a smile to their face, and I think we should take every opportunity to do so. That said, of course I want to pay special attention to a woman I am interested in, and I do not mind "looking foolish" if it looks foolish – that is what some men consider it – when you show proper etiquette to a woman. I prefer to show them respect and do little things for them than to just stand by and watch her open her own door or pull out her chair. To me, it just does not seem right. There have been many changes in the world over the years, some good and some bad, but as far as I am concerned, the disappearance of gentlemen, men who go out of their way to treat women well, is one of the bad things that have happened. I can only hope that it is true that everything comes back in style, and that sometime in the not-too-distant future, treating others with dignity and respect and showing proper etiquette will make a big comeback.

New Jersey, 58 – I grew up in Morristown, New Jersey, where my father, who was a great influence in my life, always told me that women are the most precious things on earth and I should treat them that way. From the time I started dating, I treated woman like they were precious and special. I always opened doors, pulled out chairs, walked beside them instead of in front of them, and let them see that I would be someone who would treat them special. I spent most of my adult life in the Army, so I was always surrounded by people from different states and even different countries, and unfortunately, you could see how few people treated women the same way I did. It was not an issue of race, age, or in which state they were born. It seemed that proper etiquette was just disappearing and no one cared. Even while I was married, I treated my wife the same way, and I like to think that I instilled the same values in my sons. I have two sons, thirty and twenty-eight years old, and I taught them to respect women the same way and to treat them with the proper etiquette. It appears that the younger generation has forgotten how to treat women. You just don't see the same respect and manners toward them as I used to see. I firmly believe that today's women still want a man to treat them special and with proper etiquette, even though they want to be equals in the workplace. I will never change and hope my sons will always be as they are now.

Florida, 62 – Being from the South and being an older gentleman, the practice of showing respect and courtesy and just being polite is something taught since childhood, from my parents and teachers at school. We use the terms "yes/no ma'am, yes/no sir, excuse me, please, thank you," and we hold doors for ladies and men alike, out of kindness and respect. I guess for my age group things were different. It seems to me, as we fast forward to current day, common courtesy has almost disappeared at times, from shootings to car rage, etc. In my opinion, sadly, we have become a society of "excuses," and then in amazement, we see an act of kindness and respect displayed online or in the media. We think how wonderful those actions are and see the joy it brings to us all. This is something we need to get back into our life. Well, I must say, I am an optimistic person. I believe in good things. I see a silver lining in every dark cloud. So, like in all things, someone will always shine a light of joy, bring a smile to someone's face, or a touch of happiness. Now back to being a gentleman: I think it is a grand thing, the act of showing respect to all. I have the wish that every person was a gentleperson. I truly know the world would be a better place. I believe life is a precious thing and we should all be gentlemen, showing respect to our partners, our friends, family, and our lovers! I am happy to be part of this noble project in making more aware that we are still here! "Long live the gentleman!"

Colorado, 66 – The way that I treat women (or people in general) is undoubtedly a product of the manners that both of my parents insisted on from me as a child. That said, treating everyone with respect (peers, women, and especially adults) was generally the way all kids were expected to act when I was young. Everything that I am today comes from the set of social norms that existed in our home. It didn't hurt that I was raised in a small town where everyone knew everyone and misbehavior was never a great idea. My wife taught school for a time and it seems that a lot of what is now acceptable behavior (less caring for others – too much caring for self) is reflected there. When I was in school, if I got in any sort of trouble with a teacher, the person that got the blame was me and I knew that. These days, over-caring parents (bent on depriving their children of the benefit of the experiences they will need to cope with "the world" later in life) are quick to blame the teacher or school administration – anyone but their child.

After thirty-three years of marriage I find it a pleasure to treat my wife with the respect and consideration that she truly deserves. I try not to miss a chance to open a door for her – or any opportunity to show respect (e.g. walking on the street side of the sidewalk). Showing respect for women is simply a way of demonstrating that I enjoy being a man. It's more than that though. I feel that I am a person that will go out of my way for strangers. I am not shy about assisting a complete stranger (male or female) if needed, and somehow, it makes me feel more a part of the collective humanity each time I help someone out. Just as with my wife, it is truly a pleasure to give – I think it helps me at least as much as it does the other person. The "stranger in need" and I don't know each other, but somehow we are, if only for a moment, connected. That's a good feeling.

So being a gentleman, to my wife or to a complete stranger, is all part of the same thing. It's an assertion of my manhood as much as it is an assertion that I am connected to all humans by virtue of being here on the earth and in the same place – at the same time. In marriage, it is truly the "little things" (read: thoughtfulness) that make a marriage work. My wife and I are incredibly close. After so many years of marriage, we still spend as much time together as possible and I wouldn't want it any other way. What makes the whole marriage work (love, romance, sex, friendship, the whole thing) is respect. Without respect, there is no marriage, or friendship, or anything. Showing respect to her (or to anyone) is, for me, simply an expression of my manhood – or, put another way, being a gentleman.

SUMMARY: Well, it is unanimous. Every group I have interviewed agrees on a number of issues. First, chivalry is dead! If it is not dead, it is slowly getting there. Fewer and fewer men display manners, chivalrous behavior, and simple common decency toward women. Second, everyone places the blame on women, not men. The worst argument supporting this is the feminist movement, but the point made by almost everyone interviewed, of both sexes, that women control how a man treats them, was overwhelming. The men did not hesitate to blame the women for their actions. I look at it differently: a man, a gentleman, should not even put a woman in a position to have to hint or tell the man how he should treat her. She should not have to wait at the car door until he gets the hint to open it for her. She should not have to stand by her chair while he sits down, and then wait for him to come over and pull out her chair, and she certainly should not have to give him lessons on basic table manners. I have to admit that when I started writing this book, I expected most men would blame the change on someone or something other than themselves, but I never expected that men and women alike would place all of the blame on women.

All of the men interviewed or who provided thoughts for this book agree that times have certainly changed. There were different views of how drastic the changes are, but times have changed. The older men I talked to learned it at home and feel they continue to practice what they learned from their parents and continue to mentor their children. They also agree with the women I interviewed, that women themselves can dictate how they are treated by making expectations clear and sticking to them. If they allow men to treat them poorly, then they will have to accept the results. They should realize that if a man asks them out, they are interested in spending time with them, and performing simple acts to show they are interested should not be a problem. If they are not willing to display basic etiquette, then they are probably not someone you want to be with in the first place. Usually someone shows their best side at the beginning of a relationship, so if things start out with the man not wanting to show some sort of qualities that would attract the woman, it will most likely only go downhill from there.

7.

Cultural Differences

Culture: The way of life, especially the general customs and beliefs of a particular group of people.

Today's world is more closely interconnected than ever before, and the unique American culture is being diluted or disappearing. The title of this book specifically states that I am writing about the disappearance of "The Gentleman" in America. I did so because I truly believe that the art of proper etiquette and being a gentleman is disappearing in this country. The interesting thing about how men treat women around the world is that while American men pay less attention to treating women with respect, proper treatment toward women appears to be growing stronger in other countries.

I was visiting Japan shortly after starting this book, so I was paying particular attention to the interaction between Japanese men and women. I guess I really wasn't surprised to see Japanese men treating women better than what I have seen of American men lately. The woman I interviewed in Japan talked a great deal about her culture and the past poor treatment of women by men. She stated that in the past, Japanese men were very dominant and showed little respect or appreciation toward women, in and outside of the home. The good news is that appears to be changing, and unlike in the U.S., men in Japan are actually paying more attention to women and performing those little acts that we are getting away from. As I wandered the streets of Tokyo, I noticed that men, especially younger men, were walking side by side with the woman they were with, rather than in front of them. They were opening doors and even carrying their backpacks and pushing baby strollers, things that were not very common just a few years ago. I actually was embarrassed to see countries that in the past were notorious for the way the men treated women, because it was part of the culture, showing more respect and proper etiquette than men treat women with in the U.S. As I did my research for this book and talked to women from other countries, it became quite evident that while we trend downward and treat women with less and less respect, they are trending upward and showing a much more caring attitude toward women. In this chapter, I'd like to talk a little about how men treat women in other countries. As the world grows smaller, due to social media and the ease of traveling, the odds are more likely that many men will meet women from another country whom they might be interested in socially, and it would be beneficial for you to understand their cultures.

Fortunately, I have had numerous opportunities to visit and live in several countries, and have learned a great deal about their cultures. I have found that many women from other countries who at some time or another dated and got to know an American have generally preferred to continue dating Americans. The women felt that they are treated better by American men than they are by the men from their own culture. So even though the way men treat women in America is declining at this point in time, it is still better than the treatment women receive in many other countries. Here is some general knowledge that might benefit you in the future.

Germany – Germans are more formal and punctual than most of the world. They have prescribed roles and seldom step out of line. A man or younger person should always walk to the left side of a lady. Traditional good manners call for the man to walk in front of a woman when walking into a public place. This is a symbol of protection and of the man leading the woman. A man should open the door for a woman and allow her to walk into the building, at which time the woman will stop and wait for the man. The man should then proceed to lead the woman to her destination. If going to a restaurant, the man may relinquish his leadership role to the maître d'. Don't be offended if someone corrects your behavior (i.e. taking jacket off in restaurant, parking in wrong spot, etc.). Policing each other is seen as a social duty. Compliment carefully and sparingly – it may embarrass rather than please. You don't notice too many men opening doors, picking up their dates, and paying the bill. Instead, they meet at designated places, pay for their own meals, and head home on their own.

Norway – The idea of a gentleman is something that has been basically dead in Norway as long as I can remember, and it was definitely so when I was growing up. The whole concept of a gentleman was frowned upon, because our society was focused on hyper independence of women, and the thought of chivalry and other classic gentleman gestures do not fit with the idea that women do not need men for anything. Chivalry would be an insult to our womanhood. When I was a young adult in Norway, romance was nonexistent. We did not go on dates, have candlelit dinners, or go on walks on the beach. That is not to say that Norwegians do not have romantic relationships, we do, but the way they start out are not worthy of a romance novel. The general sequence of events that led to relationships when I was a young adult was that we went to these big-town parties or festivals that are staples of Norwegian culture, we got drunk, we ended up making out with a random person, and often we'd run into them at future parties and it would happen again, and eventually a relationship would form. There were still no dates to go on. Young Norwegian couples generally hang out together at home or hang out with a group of people, generally at someone's house, instead of going out as a couple. Marriage was also not something that young people bothered with. In Norway it is perfectly acceptable to just live together without getting married, and unmarried couples who live together also have the exact same rights as a married couple, so why bother getting married. There really was no need for gentlemen in Norway. It might sound like a pretty dismal existence when it comes to relationships, but it's not that

Norwegians are just cynical and completely devoid of emotions and the need for romance. The Norwegian culture is just *extremely* laid back, and in my experience it actually takes a lot of pressure off men (and women) when it comes to relationships, because they do not have these standards of behaviors and dating etiquette that they have to live up to. Norwegian women also do not generally look down on men. It is one of the few cultures where men and women are actually equal in most senses of the word, *and* men and women actually get along pretty well! Gentlemen in Norway I believed to be a thing of the past, a concept belonging to our grandparents.

Interestingly, though, there has been a shift in Norwegian relationship culture over the last decade or so, and the concept of a gentleman has resurfaced to an extent. I believe this is due to influences from other cultures, the American one and Hollywood especially, and the rise of social media. Going on dates is suddenly a thing in Norway (and we use the English word *date* for it because we don't really have a Norwegian word for it, other than a really old-fashioned one that no one uses anymore). Men are suddenly expected to ask women out for dates, pay for dinner, celebrate Valentine's Day, and even propose! Suddenly young couples are starting to get married again! However, I would argue that chivalry is still pretty dead in Norway. I have never seen a man open a car door for a lady in the name of romance, or carry her bag, or ask her father for permission to take her hand in marriage. There might be a few exceptions, but generally we still don't see the need for gestures like that.

I believe the concept of a gentleman is basically a concept of respect. Treating your partner with respect. I don't need you to open the car door for me, I need you to take care of the kids while I go to grad school. I don't need you to ask my father for permission to marry me, I need you to respect my opinions on world events (even if you don't share them). I don't need you to pull the chair out for me when we sit down for dinner, I just need you to be faithful to me. I believe such things are much more descriptive of a true gentleman than giving flowers and carrying your shopping bags. Speaking to your partner respectfully, never putting them or their opinions down, being encouraging, supporting their dreams, treating their family and friends with respect, basically treating them the way you want to be treated. It is so simple, yet the world seems to have a really hard time with it. A little bit of romance is fun and feels good, but I believe it often ends up being nothing more than shallow gestures taking the place of much deeper needs. Respect is the key!

Asian countries – Asian countries in general are male-dominated, with vertical social structure of senior-junior/male-female relations. Family is a great part of their lives and the males are the head of family. Men are expected to possess the responsibility to provide food, clothing, and shelter to their families. Therefore, behaviors and attentions men give women are different than what they receive from American men. Women in many Asian countries do not expect to be shown any true etiquette, or to receive special treatment, and because it is not part of their culture, it is not missed. In addition, if you are traveling in Asia and meet a woman you are interested in, you should probably not make physical contact right away. It could very well make them uncomfortable because it is not normal for Asians in general to show as much physical contact in public as it is in Western culture. As I said previously, this is changing and you see many more men holding hands with and walking with their arms around women. The younger generations are treating women with more respect than the older, more traditional ones. The rest of this chapter is information provided by women from different countries, providing their thoughts and facts on how men treat women in their country. This information could be quite beneficial to a man who happens to meet a woman in one of these countries.

Japan – If you are a man who does not like treating a woman specially, and/or likes the woman to be the chivalrous one, then maybe Japan is the place for you. Japan is a male-dominated country, where there are very few expectations for men and the few that might exist during dating disappear once married, when all forms of chivalry disappear. Men do not open doors for women, they do not pull out a chair or help put on/

take off a woman's coat. When in a restaurant, you will most likely see the woman filling the man's glass when it is almost empty. Since there are no expectations when it comes to etiquette toward women, no one considers it a bad thing. It does appear that the younger generation of Japanese men is starting to change this tradition; you can now sometimes see them walking alongside the woman rather than a step or two in front of them, which has been the norm. In the past, you would very seldom see a couple holding hands in public, and you definitely would not see kissing, but times are changing and it is more commonplace to see physical contact on the street, but normally between established couples. It is still uncommon to see the older generation doing this, but as I said earlier, the trend for Japan is opposite that of the U.S., and the Japanese younger generation is starting to treat women with more respect than they traditionally have.

Korea – Most Korean men open doors for women they are dating but not car doors. Korean men do not normally pull out a woman's chair but will often wait until the woman sits down before they sit. It is possible on a special day such as an anniversary that a man might pull out a chair, but if he were to do so on a basic date, it might appear that he is just showing off, or it could lead the woman to believe that he is a player.

When walking on the street, Korean men always walk with the woman on the inside. It doesn't matter if the woman is a friend, date, or girlfriend; the man will walk to the outside. You will not see Korean men initiating holding hands or physical contact in public because the Korean culture tends not to be touchy-feely. But once they are in a serious relationship, they do tend to be a bit more open with their partner, even in public areas.

If a man and woman have just started dating and are not a "couple," the man will normally not go as far as to walk his date to the door but will wait in or by the car, watching her until she is safely inside the house. If they are in a serious relationship, the man will walk her to the door. More often than not, the woman in a new relationship will not want him to walk her to the door, because she does not feel they are at that point in the relationship yet. If that is the case, he will just have to be patient until she is ready to move to the next level.

Once they are in a relationship, Korean men tend to be much more romantic than they are when they are just starting to date someone, showing their interest by doing things such as preparing gifts for every occasion, such as an anniversary or birthday. This is not just a one-way street; the women do the same. They celebrate their anniversary by sharing gifts, but the man usually prepares a special dinner or activities to celebrate the occasion. There are many commercial events in Korea, such as Valentine's Day, White Day, Rose Day, Pepero Day (crackers), etc. Every couple doesn't celebrate each event. The specific events they celebrate and the manner in which they celebrate depend on the couple and the extent of the relationship. However, every girl is expecting to get something, at least a rose, on a special day. Men are expected to have a date on weekend nights, so normally find a woman to go out with, even if it is with a woman that he is not particularly interested in. It is merely to meet the expectations of friends and family. Once Korean men are in a relationship, they are not supposed to spend time with female friends, even if they are platonic friends from the past. There is no excuse for him to be alone with another female. He is expected to be honest, loyal, and faithful to his partner.

China – There are very few Chinese men that you would consider "gentlemen" based on Western standards. For example, less than 10% of men would open the door or walk around to open the car door for women. Of course, actions such as carrying heavy things, fixing the appliances, and changing the car tire are considered a man's job. When in a restaurant, Chinese men will wait until the woman sits down before they sit, but will not pull the chair for them. Chinese men will walk on the side of the road that protects the woman, but will very seldom hold the girl's hand while walking in public on the street; they consider it a very intimate gesture, just saved more for a loved one. Gentleman sounds exotic and high-class in China, but good Chinese men show that they care about women in a more down-to-earth way. You can't see or know Chinese men by the first glimpse if they are "gentlemen" because tradition dictates that they keep a distance and show indifference to someone they do not know very well, regardless of if it is a man or a woman. Once men are in a relationship, they take control of the relationship, not necessarily showing romance or even love but an involvement in the relationship. Chinese women keep a much lower profile. Chinese men will carry a woman's shopping bags and will go along with her even when she is shopping with girlfriends. If they have children, it is not a problem for him to stay home and watch the children. Younger Chinese men, such as those in college, also have certain cultural "rules" that they follow, such as buying and preparing gifts for every anniversary and birthday, and celebrating every special day, such as Valentine's Day or the Chinese lantern festival. In the morning you can see them carrying warm breakfast to the girl, waiting before the girl's dormitory gate, and immediately taking her books/bag so she can eat while the food is still warm. He will not leave her alone when she is mad; he will stay and comfort her until she calms down and smiles again. When going out for a date, he will give her a list of options of what they can do and she will make the final decision, instead of asking her "What would you like to do?" He also makes sure to be friends with her girlfriends but is also very careful to keep a fine distance, to ensure there is no perception of liking one of them. When talking on the phone, he always allows the woman to hang up first; he will not just cut her off and say good-night. When in a full-blown relationship, it is not uncommon for a Chinese man to share his e-mail and phone passwords to prove he has no secrets. They will get her father's permission to date his daughter. Once married, the wife is in charge of the family finances and controls the money; they even are responsible for buying their husband's clothing. Once married, they are completely dedicated to family, to include his and his wife's parents. The Chinese constitution actually stipulates that grown-up children are duty-bound to support their parents. What it all comes down to, when it comes to Chinese men, is that you will not see an elegant, passionate, romantic, funny man, but he is diligent, responsible, and reliable.

Philippines – Because the changing economy requires that more females be part of the workforce, males are becoming less dominant in the workplace, but many social rules remain. In the past, a girl brought the man who was interested in dating her home to meet her parents. Now the women are more independent, and when a man asks her out for movies and dinner, she will normally go without her parents' approval. Relationships in the Philippines have changed drastically because of modern technology and social media. Many relationships begin and grow online, via the phone, or via texting. Because of this new way to meet women, there is less patience in establishing a relationship and a lack of determination in winning a girl over. Now, the men give up on a relationship very easily and move on right away to another girl, if they are not happy with the direction the current relationship is going.

Fortunately, there are men who treat women with respect and show simple acts of kindness, such as offering a woman a seat on a crowded bus. Some men still follow the old tradition of asking a girl's parents permission to date their daughter; it is very rare, but greatly appreciated by the family. Chaperones are still occasionally used, but not nearly as often as they used to be, and dating a particular man is normally the choice of the woman and not the family. In the event she does not know the man that well and wants to feel safe and secure, she might opt to use a chaperone the first one or two dates, and in some cases, it could be a very close friend of hers. But mature men and women can go by themselves. The man is expected to pay for the dates. Also, because of the new technology, cheating on a partner is very prevalent, and though not accepted, it is expected. Because unemployment is so high in the Philippines, and the population so large, single women are easy to find, and the men have plenty of time and ways to find them. It's all part of the macho Filipino personality.

Years ago, men were expected to show respect to the parents or guardians of the girl and ask permission to court. The woman's parents or guardians would be strong and protective in order to find out his true intentions even if they liked the man. She was expected to let the man wait for a while, sometimes as long as weeks and months, before she agreed to go on a date with him or allowed him to talk to her parents.

Being a country influenced by the Spanish, they expect the male to be a gentleman, taking off his hat and politely greeting a woman on the street, or, if they are friends, walking a woman home.

They also pull out chairs when dining, open doors for them, and walk on the curb side to protect the woman from accidents. A Filipina woman does not normally say straightforwardly what she wants. When married and at home, the man is very dominant. He expects to have food ready on the table when he gets home from work. He does not do household chores such as cooking, laundry, cleaning the house, and taking care of the children. In general, a Filipino man is affectionate, passionate, and romantic during dating, but becomes much more dominant once married.

Thailand – Thai men can be shy. You can chat with a Thai man all evening, swap phone numbers, and still not be sure if you're just friends or if there is more of an interest. They will be sweet, attentive, and charming, and you still can't figure out if it's just social conventions that make them behave so nonchalantly, but they want to take you for dinner. They're slow and shy in their approach and they might not even make one. But don't necessarily mistake his lack of aggressiveness for disinterest. Make it clear that you like him, but don't throw yourself at him. Smile at him a lot. Don't flirt with other guys.

Though this is a common dating rule amongst most societies, it's strongly recommended that if you want to keep a Thai guy, don't sleep with him on the first date. Western girls are sometimes viewed as more promiscuous than Thai girls, so let him know right up front that you are interested in getting to know him and that you are not just looking for a fling. Pay half the bill on your first date; this will make it clear that you want to be treated like an equal.

Many girls say that Thai men can be incredibly romantic and treat you like a queen at the start of the relationship. This may not always last, but hey, enjoy it while it does! Be a bit mysterious. Don't give away everything about yourself when you first start dating. Remain confident, and if he does something that you think would be unacceptable, make it known to him without getting angry, but be sure to point it out rather than internalizing it. He may turn you down the first few times you invite him into your bedroom. This is part of Thai culture, and his way of showing respect for you. Embrace it – how cute is that!? He'll come in eventually...

Many girls have experienced the hot-and-cold nature of the Thai man they're dating. They may inexplicably not call, or ignore you for a while, and then turn up all lovey-dovey. On the other hand, they could become overzealous and call you five or more times a day. Be aware of it, and it's up to you whether you can deal with it or not. He may call you fat. This is an obvious no-no in the West, but in Thailand, calling someone fat is not seen as offensive. Most Thai women are around forty kilograms, so compared to that, most Western women are quite a bit bigger. Try not to take too much offense, but let him know that you don't like it when he says that. Some Thai boyfriends get insanely jealous and possessive. Some even threaten rival men with bodily harm. Don't provoke this jealousy or you could get someone seriously hurt. If you really like him and want to keep him, show copious amounts of respect for his family – he respects them much more than he lets on. If you get to meet his family (he will be eager for this to happen if he likes you), try to be as polite as you can without relinquishing your personality. Dress ultra-conservatively when meeting his family. His grandma will not appreciate your stellar cleavage.

Speaking of which, in general, try not to wear clothes that are too revealing around him. This means showing extra patience, femininity, and sweetness (do your best not to argue with him or yell at him), but also carrying your own handbag, and being able to hold and buy your own drinks. Allow him his freedom – let him go out with his friends and don't always drag him out with yours.

Thais tend to offer up the word *love* much quicker than might be expected in the West. Expect and know this, and judge for yourself on how seriously you want to take it. Be aware that infidelity is not necessarily frowned upon in Thailand. Many Thai men (and women as well) have more than one girlfriend. If you're not cool with that, make it known from the beginning, and watch for signs without being overly paranoid. At the end of the day, the lifestyle differences may be too much. If it gets that way, but you're not sure how to end it, here is one phrase suggested: "I love you, but as much as I try, it's not in the way that you deserve." However, that's not always the case. So it's probably just down to the individual in the end.

SUMMARY: So, as you can see, although there are many differences from culture to culture, respect for women is increasing in most countries. Although we tend to still treat women better than men in many other countries, the trends are opposite. Treatment of women in the U.S. is in a downward spiral, while men in many other countries are treating women better than ever before. This is one change that is not positive. The good thing is, it is not difficult to change. The change does not take money or possessions; it just takes a little effort.

8.

Where Do We Go From Here?

Expectations: The belief of what might or could happen in the future.

So where does this leave us? We are in a downward spiral in so many ways when it comes to society and how we treat one another, not only on dates but just in general. What happened to saying "excuse me" when you bump into someone, or apologizing for making a mistake? It appears now that it is beneath people to acknowledge that they have done something wrong, so it is easier to just walk away without saying anything, or just blame it on the other person. Although I concentrate on treating women with dignity and respect and proper etiquette throughout the book, the problem is deeper than that.

I have talked to numerous men and women while writing this book, and the common belief is, the way men treat women has negatively changed over the years. When you talk to younger women, they do not really recognize it as an issue because they are not aware of how well men treated women fifteen or twenty years ago. However, the older women I interviewed would talk about the "old days." They would emphasize how men no longer treated women with respect. They said that they missed experiencing and seeing how men used to treat women. Across the board, regardless of age, they all thought that women should be treated with respect, regardless of the type of relationship they were involved in.

So where do we go from here? How do we get back to a society where men treat women with the dignity and respect they deserve, not just while on a date, but under any circumstances? When will we see men once again stopping to help a woman carrying a heavy box or hold a door open for a complete stranger? How do we once again bring back manners and etiquette that seem to have disappeared? How do we bring back "The Gentleman"?

MEN – You see movies all of the time where the underdog, a high school or college student, falls for a girl who they feel is way out of their league. In order to overcome their shortcomings, they do something nice or even wacky to get her attention. Well, this situation is not uncommon. Movies are not made every time the underdog gets the girl, but it does give hope to those young men who encounter a similar situation. It takes one gesture at the right time to get a woman's attention, and if you do that, you have opened the door to endless possibilities. It could be as simple as complimenting her shoes or some other small gesture that makes her notice you.

I can say this because I met one of the most important people in my life because of just this kind of situation. While I was working in Japan, there was a beautiful woman whom I noticed wandering around the building where I worked, but I never had the opportunity to speak with her and it appeared that she did not know I was alive. She was beautiful, always nice and polite to everyone, had a smile every hour of the day, and dressed impeccably. One day, we happened to attend the same conference. The weather outside was warm but the room was cool because of the air conditioning. I noticed that she had her arms crossed and was rubbing them. I left the conference room, found a coat, and offered it to her. That was eight years ago, and we are as close as any two people can be. Had I not made that simple gesture, we may have never talked, and I would have lost out on someone who will forever be an important part of my life. What is so difficult about showing this etiquette toward someone you care about or are at least interested in?

As I said previously, being a gentleman costs you nothing but can pay great dividends. If you treat a date this way, you can possibly win the heart of a prospective partner, and you can earn the respect of female friends and business associates. You could also be the role model to other men who see your actions. Remember, in the case of a date: if you thought enough of her to ask her out, why wouldn't you want to do whatever necessary to impress her? Especially when you know that it will give you a huge advantage over other men who might not be interested enough to treat her specially? Common sense should tell you that all things being equal, a woman is normally going to choose a man who treats her well, whom she is comfortable with and feels safe and secure with. You are showing her these attributes. When she sees over time that she can expect this type of treatment from you, that you were not just doing it to impress her on the first date, you have made an impression that will be hard for someone else to top. You can and should treat your female platonic friends the same way. It allows them to experience the same gentlemanly behavior you show your partner, and hopefully influences them to set higher standards for and expectations from men they go out with, and, in some cases, increases their self-confidence and self-respect. One person at a time, this is the way that we can help bring the gentleman back into play.

I am a believer in the idea of performing at least one nice act for someone every single day, something that will bring a smile to their face. It can be something as simple as holding the door open for a stranger to complimenting someone on their hair or what they are wearing – not in an inappropriate way that will have the person running in the opposite direction or spraying mace into your face. Recently, I was on an airplane on a seven-hour flight. As we departed, I noticed a woman traveling alone with a child that could not have been more than three months old. She was holding the child on her lap. An hour into the flight, I turned to her and stated that if she had to go to the bathroom during the flight, I would be more than happy to hold her child for her, that I had two children of my own and could handle that task for a few minutes. We shared a laugh and she thanked me. About two hours later, I felt a tap on my shoulder and she asked if I would hold her child for a few minutes. I would like to think that my making the offer was a relief for her because she didn't have to ask the awkward question later, or try to hold things in – the entire trip.

I would say that not a day goes by that we do not have a number of opportunities to be a good person or a gentleman. If you are paying a woman a compliment, say what you have to say and keep walking; don't make it appear that you are trying to pick her up or have ulterior motives, or it will take away from the purpose of the compliment. You will be surprised how often a simple act or compliment can change someone's day. Acts of kindness do not always have to be directed toward a woman. There is nothing wrong with paying a compliment to another man. As I state throughout this book, it costs you nothing to be nice to people, to show some manners, to be a gentleman. Just performing a simple act of kindness might allow you to make new friends, initiate a new relationship, and gain new respect and admiration from those that you already know, who witness and approve of your actions. Your actions could also drive others to start doing the same thing. One person changing at a time can eventually lead to a major shift in our society.

LADIES – I hate to put a burden on your shoulders, but unfortunately I must. The road to change involves you. You alone set the standard, and you alone ensure it is met. Women often stated that as they grow older, it becomes harder to find a good man for a meaningful relationship, that they lower the bar as to expectations from a partner, and just settle, rather than find their "soul mate," or at least a good man, who will treat them the way they wish to be treated.

One of the many questions raised while I was writing this book is…have men consciously made the decision to treat women with less manners, or have women lowered their expectations and are now willing to accept less from men? If the latter is true, then it may be just as simple to reverse the current negative trend as putting your foot down and raising expectations again. Demand the treatment that you deserve. Everyone knows the saying that everything comes back around eventually, whether it be hairstyles or clothes. Maybe it is time for etiquette toward women to come back around, since it has been in this death spiral for so long.

Think about it: a man asks you out because he is interested in you. That being the case, you have the control and therefore the ability to dictate the path forward. Regardless of age, whether you are eighteen and just starting to date, or divorced and getting back into the dating scene, when you are on the first date with someone, you have the power to set all expectations for the relationship. Let your expectations be known. Let him know that you are a lady and expect to be treated as one. If he picks you up in a car and does not open the door for you, stand there until he gets the hint and comes around and opens it. If you are entering a building and he does not open the door for you, let it close and stand outside the door until he gets the hint and comes back and holds open the door for you. I assure you, it will not take him long to get the hint. It might be a bit embarrassing, but it shows him how you expect to be treated. You have now established your expectations and let him know that if he wants to continue seeing you, he will have to meet them. This is also the way that you can weed out those men who are really interested in you and getting to know you from those with other intentions.

Don't just stop with insisting your partner or date opens your door and pulls out your chairs; this is the time to let a man know your expectations. Let him know if you would like him to fill your water glass when it is empty. Let him know you would like him to walk on the correct side of you when walking down the street. Set your expectations high and make them clear to him from the beginning. If you make him aware of your expectations from the beginning, you will learn very quickly how interested he is in you, because he will have to make the conscious decision based on your expectations. If he wants to get to know you, he will not hesitate to treat you the way you desire to be treated. If he refuses to adhere to your desires, then he most likely is not the kind of man you are looking for. In most cases, he will meet your expectations, even if you have set the bar higher than he is used to. Ladies, if you do not take the lead and let the men in your life know your expectations, a change for the better will never come, and you can bet that fewer and fewer men will know how to treat a lady.

EVERYONE – We all should be role models, especially for our children. In most cases, the way people behave when they are adults is based on their surroundings as they grow up. As I have previously mentioned, it is all about past experience, and that normally begins at home. So if you can make this part of your lifestyle, there is a good chance that your son will grow up treating women with the same dignity and respect as his male role model in the home and that your daughter will have the same expectations as her female role model in the house and be attracted to men who treat her the same.

I originally intended to avoid this subject, but since I have talked about influences, I guess it only makes sense to talk about external influences such as movies and music. There is a chance that if it is acceptable for your children to grow up watching movies that show violence towards women or mistreatment in general, then they will act the same, because they have no way of knowing that it is unacceptable behavior. The same goes for music that disrespects women and endorses violence or mistreatment of women. Obviously, you cannot monitor what your children watch or listen to every day, especially as they grow older, but you can ensure that they are raised to understand the difference between good and bad behavior. More importantly, you can reinforce the fact that the type of "entertainment" that shows the mistreatment of women is not acceptable and is only made to create controversy and make money.

So it is up to all of us to bring back those basic manners and etiquette that were so prevalent just twenty years ago. It will not be an easy change, but it is possible. The change can happen one person at a time and one generation at a time. It can reappear in our society, the same way it has been disappearing. If we don't start working in this direction, if men don't show respect to women and women continue to set low standards and have low expectations of the men in their lives, it will just be a matter of time before we will experience the total disappearance of THE GENTLEMAN.

Made in the USA
Columbia, SC
24 November 2017